Model Drawing *for* Challenging Word Problems

Finding Solutions the Singapore Way

Lorraine Walker

Crystal Springs
SDE BOOKS

a division of Staff Development for Educators

Peterborough, New Hampshire

Published by Crystal Springs Books
A division of Staff Development for Educators (SDE)
10 Sharon Road, PO Box 500
Peterborough, NH 03458
1-800-321-0401
www.SDE.com/crystalsprings

Published 2010
Printed in the United States of America
14 13 12 11 10   1 2 3 4 5

ISBN: 978-1-934026-98-4

Library of Congress Cataloging-in-Publication Data

Walker, Lorraine, 1946-
    Model drawing for challenging word problems : finding solutions the Singapore way / Lorraine
        Walker.
        p. cm.
    Includes index.
    ISBN 978-1-934026-98-4
    1. Problem solving--Study and teaching (Middle school)--Singapore. 2. Word problems
        (Mathematics)--Study and teaching (Middle school)--Singapore. 3. Mathematics--Study and
        teaching (Middle school)--United States. I. Title.

QA63.W35 2010
372.7--dc22

                                        2010007814

Editor: Sharon Smith
Art Director and Designer: S. Dunholter
Production Coordinator: Deborah Fredericks
Illustrator: S. Dunholter

I dedicate this book to Char Forsten. We started this Singapore Math journey together, and I've enjoyed every bit of the ride with you.

And I dedicate it to Dr. Yeap Ban Har. Through your example, you showed me a better way to question kids and to encourage them to be thinkers.

Contents

Acknowledgments

I have had the opportunity to work with some dedicated and passionate math people since I started studying math strategies from Singapore. In addition to Char Forsten and Dr. Yeap Ban Har, I want to thank four others who have been part of this journey since the beginning.

Anni Stipek always has a smile on her face—even when asked to use her keen eyes to proof these problems (multiple times!) to ensure their accuracy.

Sandy Chen, Catherine Kuhns, and Jana Hazekamp have, through all their sharing and support, indirectly helped me write this book.

And finally, though these two people probably never thought of themselves as mathematicians, I wish to thank Sharon Smith, editor, and Soosen Dunholter, art director and book designer on this project. Both have passed the final exam and, most likely, could teach model drawing now.

Thank you to all for being supportive colleagues and my good friends.

Introduction

Why do we ask kids to solve word problems?

My answer to this question would be that we teach word problems to help develop students who are thinkers. We want them to be able to look at a problem, analyze it, and decide the best approach to take to solve it.

Model drawing can get kids there.

I still remember the first time I saw for myself what a difference model drawing could make in a math class. Char Forsten and I were visiting a fifth-grade class in Massachusetts that had been working with model drawing and other Singapore Math strategies. As we watched students solve word problems that seemed way beyond their grade level, Char and I kept looking at each other and saying, "Oh, my." What impressed us was that these students weren't just rattling off answers. They really understood the concepts.

Since that day, I've often thought that I'd like to round up all my former students and tell them to meet me back in Room 212 so I can teach them a better way to solve word problems. I can picture the looks on their faces after I showed them these techniques from Singapore, and I can assure you there would be more eyes lighting up than I ever saw before.

You know who would love model drawing the most? Jerry.

A Lesson in Unintended Consequences

Jerry was a boy with very curly red hair who sat in the back of the room. He rarely contributed anything during class discussions but did quite well on tests and quizzes. Like some others, he usually just wrote down his answers without showing any of his work. I actually thought Jerry might be cheating on those quizzes. He was about to prove me wrong.

One day I handed out a quiz with the answers already filled in. The class nearly freaked out. (A little later, some parents did, too.) I told my students I didn't care whether they used the procedure we'd been studying, but before I would give anyone credit for solving a problem, they had to show me, in writing, how they got to the answer. I thought for sure this would show me whether those students who weren't showing their work were actually cheating.

Well, guess what? Jerry hadn't been cheating. Once I changed the quiz rules, he would often draw a diagram or picture to illustrate his thinking. His visuals made it pretty clear what his thought process was and how he'd gone about solving the problem. His test scores continued to be among the best in the class.

I decided to follow Jerry's lead. I realized from students' reactions that word problems seemed to be more engaging and clearer if I added drawings as we worked out the solutions on the board. Some of my drawings for those problems could have won prizes. That didn't matter. What did matter was that I could see how those visuals improved kids' understanding of the math. And that's what model drawing does.

Building a Bridge

In *Step-by-Step Model Drawing,* Char Forsten writes, "The goal of model drawing is to build a pictorial bridge to abstract thinking." What a great goal. Starting with the simplest problem used in the early primary grades, model drawing builds that bridge to abstract thinking and algebra. Don't get me wrong—my ultimate goal is to get kids to cross that bridge and to be able to solve problems algebraically. But model drawing is wonderful for kids who are struggling with abstract math, because it literally gives them a picture of what's happening in the problem. It gives the problems meaning. And it provides a life preserver should kids fall off the bridge and need a little support.

Model drawing gives word problems a visual context. Students translate the words and numbers in the problems into what is basically a graphic organizer that shows relationships among numbers. Problems that were once too wordy, too complicated, or too abstract can now be shown as clear, well-organized visuals. (This process isn't appropriate for every problem, so you still need to teach other problem-solving strategies. Often, though, model drawing is a great way to go.) And aside from the fact that using these problem-solving techniques will improve kids' math scores, probably the most amazing thing about model drawing is that it will help your students start enjoying math instead of dreading math.

Extending the Bridge

If you've tried model drawing with your students, you already know how well it works when kids are beginning to solve word problems. In this book, I want to show you ways you can kick things up a notch.

I've tried to make sure that every problem in this book falls into one or more of these categories:

1. It's similar to problems found in U.S. math textbooks for grades six through nine.

2. To solve it, you have to go beyond basic model drawing and think in a more complex way.

3. It can be solved using slightly more advanced model-drawing techniques. (This includes before-and-after problems and other problems that call for multiple-step solutions.)

4. It creates a good transition to solving word problems using algebraic equations.

Be Patient

I do have one caution for you: be patient. It took a lot of practice for me to get my brain rewired so that I didn't try to solve every word problem algebraically. I think it's like learning a new language. There's a point at which you no longer have to first translate the foreign language to English before you can understand it. That's how it worked for me with model drawing.

How to Use This Book

I've set this book up so you can use it in several different ways. I hope you'll try solving each problem on your own before you look at the suggested solution. If you get stuck, look at the drawing. (The drawing doesn't show how the model would look after you finished solving the problem. It shows how you might want to *set up* the model. It should be just enough to get you going.) After that, read my comments. That's where I give you a look inside my head as I decide the approach I'll take to solve the problem. Finally, because model drawing also gives you a lot of chances for questioning and finding out what kids are thinking, I've included some ideas for doing that.

Of course, we're not all going to approach these problems the same way, so don't be concerned if your thinking isn't the same as mine. One of the great things about Singapore Math is that it teaches kids there's more than one way to look at a problem. My thoughts are there only in case you need them.

The Real Challenge

I used to have kids in my classes who would say, "My parents can't do math either." I'd always think, "Why is that an acceptable thing to say?" Those same students never went around saying, "My parents can't read either." Math has historically been a challenge for many people, and I think I know at least part of the reason for that. Though colleges in the United States usually offer many classes on how to teach reading and writing, rarely does a school have more than one or two classes on how to teach math. And if those classes don't cover how to make math meaningful and comprehensible, you (the future teacher) are out of luck.

When I first started teaching, I wanted kids to translate each problem into an algebraic equation and solve the equation. If they got the right answer, we were both happy. If I was covering a lesson on dividing fractions and a student said "I don't get it," I'd say, "Just flip-flop and multiply." I taught the way I'd been taught, and I think most of us do that.

"Flip-flop and multiply" does not explain the math.

If we want kids to start liking, learning, and understanding math, we have to change how we teach math. I hope this book will help you to do that.

Word Problems

Whole Numbers

Maria and Carlos each can earn $12 a day walking dogs. If they start with $25 and $14 respectively, and they both work every day, in how many days will their combined earnings equal $159?

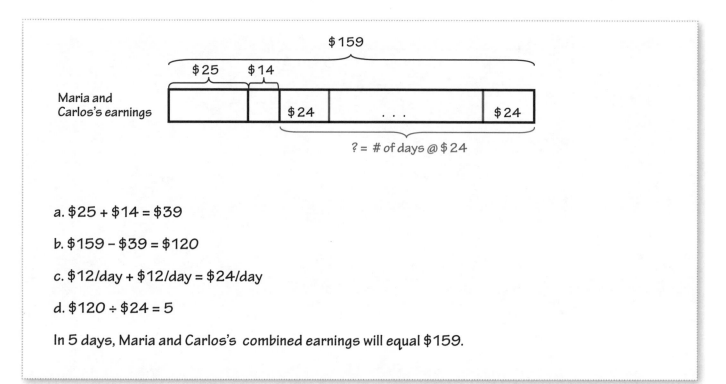

a. $25 + $14 = $39

b. $159 − $39 = $120

c. $12/day + $12/day = $24/day

d. $120 ÷ $24 = 5

In 5 days, Maria and Carlos's combined earnings will equal $159.

This problem is an example of a quotitive division problem, in which you know the number of items in a group (in this case, $24) and you need to know how many groups are in the total (in this case, 5). The computation that's required is division.

By the way, if you give this problem (or any problem) to your students, try substituting student names for the ones in the original problem. It's a great way to get students engaged.

Another Way

The first model you draw may not always be the one you ulti-
mately use to solve the problem. When I started to work on this
problem, I drew a comparison model like the one shown here.

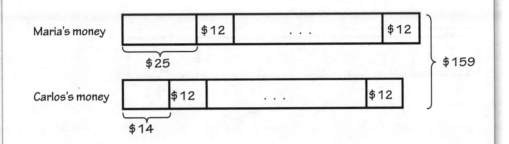

? = number of days @ $12

That would be a perfectly acceptable solution, but then I realized it might not be the easiest one. Instead, I decided to com-
bine what I knew about Maria's earnings and what I knew about
Carlos's earnings. That let me use the part-whole model, which
seemed to me to be clearer for this particular problem.

Almost all word problems are either part-whole problems or
comparison problems. Occasionally you'll find one like this one
that can be solved either way.

Whole Numbers

For every $2 Kendra spent on materials, she could make 5 coasters. She made 60 coasters and sold them at the York Beach Fair, charging $5 for 2 coasters. What was her profit?

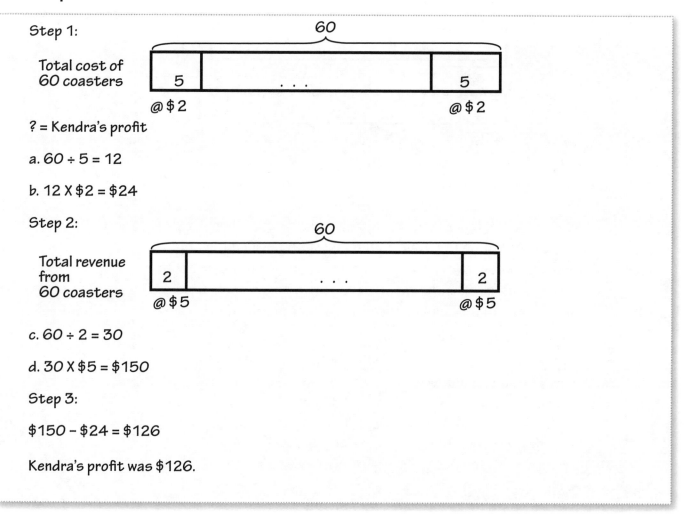

Step 1:

Total cost of 60 coasters

60

5   . . .   5

@ $2   @ $2

? = Kendra's profit

a. 60 ÷ 5 = 12

b. 12 X $2 = $24

Step 2:

Total revenue from 60 coasters

60

2   . . .   2

@ $5   @ $5

c. 60 ÷ 2 = 30

d. 30 X $5 = $150

Step 3:

$150 – $24 = $126

Kendra's profit was $126.

This is another quotitive division problem, but with an added twist. This problem includes multiple values—not only the number of coasters but also the expenses and revenue associated with those coasters. Breaking the problem into multiple steps like this seems to keep it pretty clear. I use this approach a lot—not only for myself but also as a way to chunk a lot of information into smaller, more manageable pieces for the kids.

What's not so clear is where the question mark should go. In a case like this, I just write "? =" below the model. That still reminds me exactly what I'm looking for, even when the question mark doesn't fit neatly into the model.

A rope is divided into 3 pieces. One piece is 3 inches longer than the shortest piece and 5 inches shorter than the longest piece. If the total of the combined pieces is 92 inches, how long is each piece?

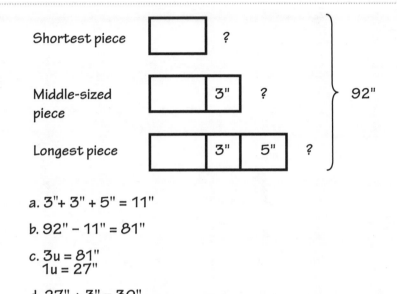

a. 3" + 3" + 5" = 11"

b. 92" − 11" = 81"

c. 3u = 81"
   1u = 27"

d. 27" + 3" = 30"

e. 27" + 3" + 5" = 35"

The rope pieces are 27 inches, 30 inches, and 35 inches.

I like this problem because it shows how, even when a problem is really wordy, translating it to a visual model can make finding the solution a piece of cake.

To solve this word problem, kids need a solid understanding of the concept of "more vs. less." I would recommend that before you give students this problem, you build background knowledge. The lesson might go something like this.

Suppose we have 2 ropes, and we start out assuming they are equal in length.

Rope A

Rope B

Now suppose we learn that Rope B is 5 inches longer than Rope A. How should we adjust the model to show that?

Most kids will probably suggest this:

If no one suggests another alternative, you need to push them a little. Tell them you really don't want to change Rope B's unit bar, so any change they make needs to be to Rope A's bar. Keep discussing options. (Does Rope A need to be bigger or smaller than Rope B?) Someone should suggest this:

It's very important for kids to understand this option, so be sure to spend plenty of time on it. Perseverance and good questioning are key to developing strong mathematicians.

Whole Numbers

Mary had saved $117, but her sister Suzanne had saved only $36. After they both earned the same amount of money washing dishes one weekend, Mary noticed she had twice as much money as Suzanne. What was the combined total they earned by doing dishes?

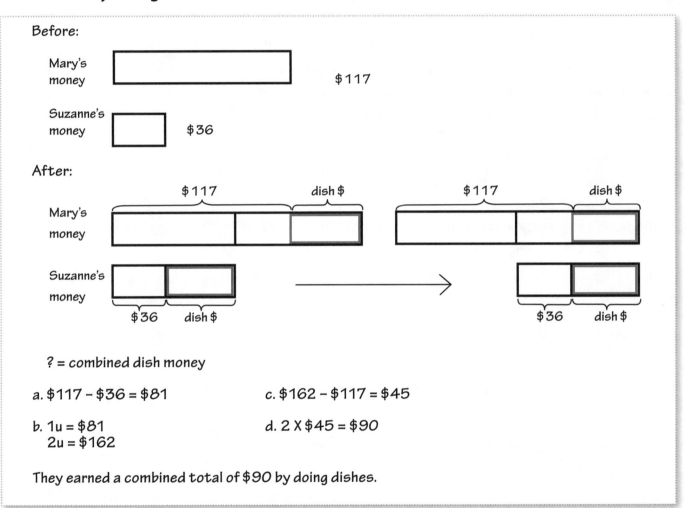

? = combined dish money

a. $117 – $36 = $81

c. $162 – $117 = $45

b. 1u = $81
   2u = $162

d. 2 X $45 = $90

They earned a combined total of $90 by doing dishes.

This is a before-and-after problem. In this type of problem, the relationship between 2 quantities is given, but then some change occurs and the relationship changes. In this case the change was that both Mary's and Suzanne's savings increased after they earned more money.

The "After" model for this problem was a bit tricky, and initially I couldn't see what computation I could do. But then I did 2 things that made my model much clearer.

The first thing I did was to add color. In the "After" model I knew Mary's money was twice Suzanne's. But it wasn't until I added the red box to show their recent earnings that things started to come into focus.

The second thing I did was to slide the unit bars to the right. Since I'd put each of the red boxes on the right end of its unit bar, I realized it would be easier for me to compare them if one was directly over the other. So I slid Suzanne's bar to the right and added the proper quantity labels. Voilà! Things started making sense.

If you're not sure what to do with a problem, consider making some changes like these. There's no rule that says how the unit bars need to line up or how many colors you can use to draw the model. (Go a little easy on the color, though. Too many colors or too much color means you're no longer highlighting anything.)

Rolff is now 4 years older than Erik. Five years ago Rolff was twice as old as Erik. How old was Rolff 5 years ago?

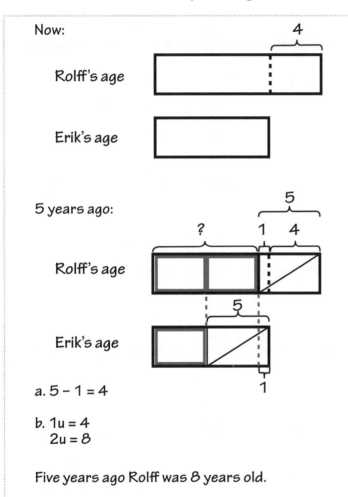

Now:

Rolff's age

Erik's age

4

5 years ago:

5

?   1   4

Rolff's age

5

Erik's age

1

a. 5 – 1 = 4

b. 1u = 4
   2u = 8

Five years ago Rolff was 8 years old.

Age problems are typically just another version of before-and-after problems. In an age problem, what changes is the year. You're comparing 2 people's ages now, and then you're looking at how that relationship will have changed a few years from now—or some variation on that theme.

Before you start this problem with your kids, you might want to lay a little groundwork. It would be great if you could use 2 kids in your class to be your "models." Let's assume your models are Liam and Tanya. Tell them you're going to pretend that Liam is 12 and Tanya is 15. Have them stand up and answer your questions, so you can fill in the chart on the next page.

	Now	3 Years Ago	6 Years from Now
Liam's age	12	9	18
Tanya's age	15	12	21

Now let's use this chart to dig deeper into the comparisons between their ages. The conversation might go something like this:

What is the difference between your ages now? 3 years.

What was the difference between your ages 3 years ago? 3 years.

What will be the difference between your ages 6 years from now? 3 years.

Hmm. Does it matter what time I pick, or will you always be 3 years apart? Always 3 years apart.

What's the ratio of Liam's age to Tanya's age now? 4 : 5

What was the ratio of Liam's age to Tanya's age 3 years ago? 3 : 4

What will the ratio of Liam's age to Tanya's age be 6 years from now? 6 : 7

Hmm. So the difference between your ages remained constant, but when you compared your ages at different times the ratio changed.

If you really want to push the kids, ask them: *Do you think there could ever be another time when the ratio of your ages could be, say, 3 : 4 again?*

This last question should get them thinking. If anyone comes up with an answer, let me know. I used some algebra and set up the following ratio:

Liam's age = x
Tanya's age = $x + 3$

$$\frac{x}{x + 3} = \frac{3}{4}$$

The only solution for x was $x = 9$, so it appears the ratio of their ages would be 3 : 4 only when they were 9 and 12 years old.

The whole point to this "pregame" activity is to get kids to see that Rolff's and Erik's ages are always going to be 4 years apart, but the *relationship* between their ages changes over time.

The greatest of 4 consecutive integers is 22. Find the sum of the 4 integers.

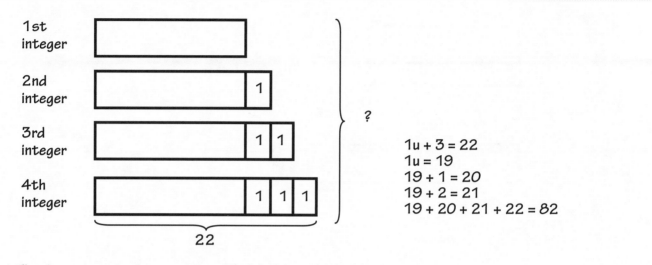

1st integer

2nd integer

3rd integer · 1 1

4th integer · 1 1 1

?

1u + 3 = 22
1u = 19
19 + 1 = 20
19 + 2 = 21
19 + 20 + 21 + 22 = 82

22

The 4 consecutive integers are 19, 20, 21, and 22. Their sum is 82.

This is really an easy problem. Some kids will solve it immediately just by starting with the value of the greatest integer (22) and working backward to find the others. It's a good problem to use early on, though, because it gives you a chance to reinforce what "consecutive integers" means and what the visual model needs to show.

Another Way

Some students may prefer to show consecutive numbers in the model by drawing 1 unit bar, that unit bar plus 1, the same unit bar plus 2, and finally the unit bar plus 3—like this.

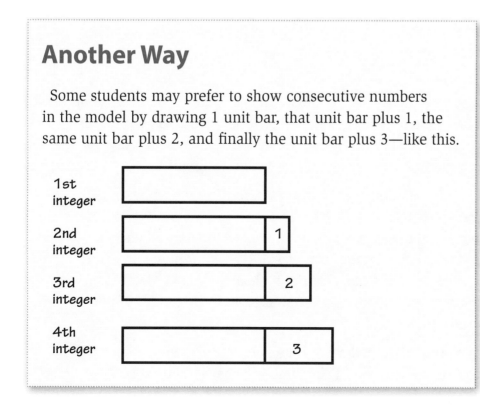

1st integer

2nd integer · 1

3rd integer · 2

4th integer · 3

Whole Numbers

The sum of 3 consecutive odd integers is 57. Find the integers.

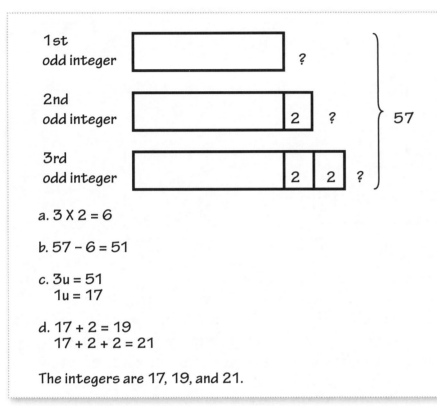

a. 3 X 2 = 6

b. 57 – 6 = 51

c. 3u = 51
   1u = 17

d. 17 + 2 = 19
   17 + 2 + 2 = 21

The integers are 17, 19, and 21.

In order to set up and solve this problem, the student must already understand that consecutive odd (and even) integers differ by 2.

I've had students who solved this problem using averages. They knew that in any group of 3 consecutive numbers, the middle number has to be the average of the 3. They computed the average, and then they just subtracted 2 to get the least number and added 2 to get the greatest number. I say, if they can come up with other clever ways to solve a problem like this, more power to them!

If students do go this route, ask them whether they could use the same technique if the problem were about 4 consecutive odd or even numbers. While you're at it, question them about the sums of even and odd consecutive numbers. Ask, "What if my original problem had said the sum was 56? Without doing any computations, would you have seen a red flag that I'd made a mistake?" Make them tell you why. (You want them to explain that the sum of an odd number of odd integers will always be odd.)

Now suppose the original problem had said, "The sum of 3 consecutive even integers is 54." Any red flags on this one? (This time the answer should be "no.")

Whole Numbers

The greater of 2 consecutive even integers is 18 less than 3 times the smaller integer. What is the greater integer?

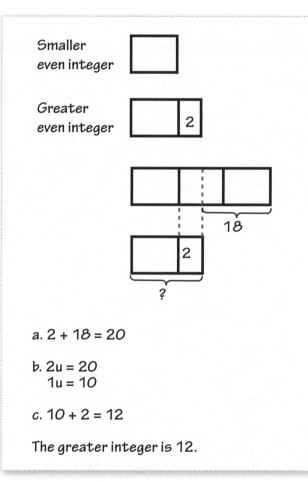

Smaller even integer

Greater even integer

18

2

?

a. 2 + 18 = 20

b. 2u = 20
    1u = 10

c. 10 + 2 = 12

The greater integer is 12.

The prior knowledge needed to solve this problem is that if the 2 integers are consecutive even integers, then they differ by 2. Understanding that, I know when I place the 18 in the model that the value of the space between that portion and the portion that's equal to the smaller number will be only 2. This is a good time to emphasize that when we say the greater integer is 2 more than the smaller one, that means the same thing as saying that they differ by 2.

The 3 angles of a triangle are consecutive even numbers. How big is each angle?

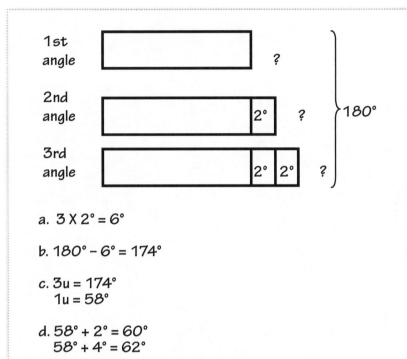

a. $3 \times 2° = 6°$

b. $180° - 6° = 174°$

c. $3u = 174°$
   $1u = 58°$

d. $58° + 2° = 60°$
   $58° + 4° = 62°$

The angles of the triangle are 58°, 60°, and 62°.

The prior knowledge needed to solve this problem is that the 3 angles of a triangle add up to 180°—and of course, once again, that consecutive even numbers differ by 2.

Another Way

Some clever student may use averaging to solve this problem. She might find the average of the 3 numbers, subtract 2 to find the least number, and add 2 to find the greatest number. If somebody suggests this approach, be sure to ask her to explain her reasoning and then congratulate her on thinking outside the box. (If no one suggests this alternative approach, ask your students if they think it could be used—and how.)

The sum of 5 consecutive integers is 12 more than 4 times the fourth integer. What are the numbers?

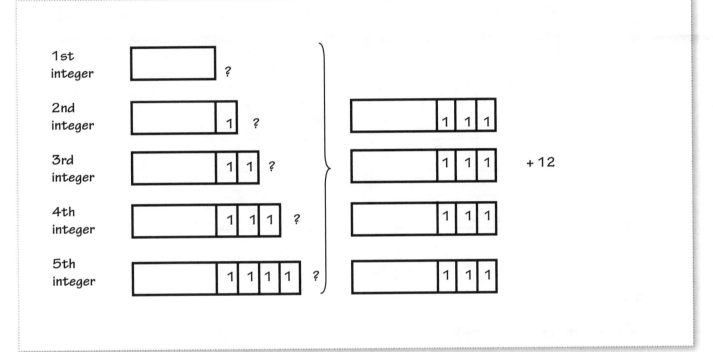

This solution came from my colleague Bill Hayo and his middle-grade class in Arizona. The left-hand side of the "equation" represents the sum of the consecutive integers, and the right-hand side shows "4 times the fourth integer." (Since multiplication is the same as repeated addition, the right-hand side shows "4 times the fourth integer" by repeating—adding—that integer 4 times.) Notice how this drawing uses the brace as the equivalent of an equal sign.

What Bill's class is doing is treating the model as a balance scale. Once they set up the drawing like this, they start crossing off the unknown unit bars from each side of the brace, always crossing off 1 unit on the right for every 1 they cross off on the left. They do the same thing with the single-digit units. After they finish all the crossing out, they're left with 1 unknown unit on the left side and 2 single-digit units plus the 12 on the right side—something like the marked-up model on the next page.

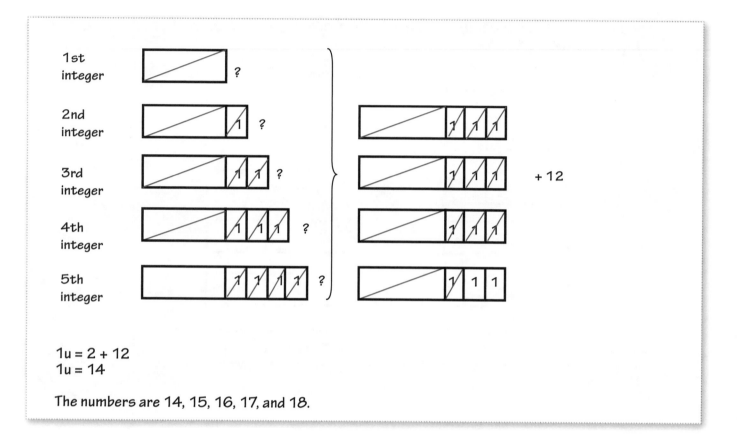

1st integer

2nd integer

3rd integer

4th integer

5th integer

1u = 2 + 12
1u = 14

The numbers are 14, 15, 16, 17, and 18.

Clever people, those Arizona folks!

Whole Numbers

Measured in inches, the widths of 4 quilts are consecutive multiples of 3. If the 4 quilts are placed side by side, their combined width is 198 inches. What is the width of the widest of the 4 quilts?

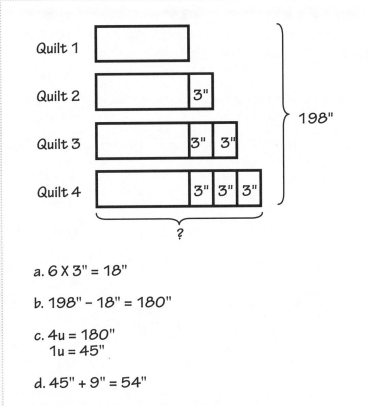

a. 6 X 3" = 18"

b. 198" – 18" = 180"

c. 4u = 180"
    1u = 45"

d. 45" + 9" = 54"

The widest quilt is 54 inches wide.

The prior knowledge needed for this problem is an understanding that if you have numbers that are consecutive multiples of 3, each number will be 3 more than the previous number. Beyond that, you can solve this problem in the same way you'd solve any other consecutive number problem.

PROBLEM 12

Four people at work were born on consecutive days in July. The sum of the 4 dates is 86. On what dates do their birthdays fall?

PROBLEM 13

Jan shopped at 4 different stores. When she looked at her receipts, she realized that the amounts she had spent in the 4 stores were consecutive multiples of 7. The total amount she spent was $98 more than twice what she spent at the second store. How much did Jan spend at the second store?

PROBLEM 14

The lengths of the sides of a quadrilateral are consecutive multiples of 6. If the perimeter of the quadrilateral is 156 inches, how long is the shortest side?

Gail had more money than Tracy when they left for vacation. After Gail spent $\frac{3}{8}$ of her money and Tracy spent $32, they each had the same amount left. If they had a total of $422 when they started, how much did Tracy have after vacation?

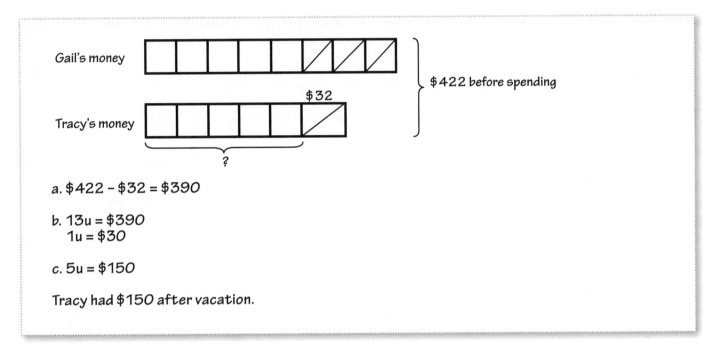

a. $422 − $32 = $390

b. 13u = $390
   1u = $30

c. 5u = $150

Tracy had $150 after vacation.

Sometimes model drawing involves a bit of trial and error. When I first tried to solve this problem, I set up the bars as above but then, to represent what Gail spent, crossed out the 3 units of hers that were farthest to the left. The problem became so much easier to visualize when I tried crossing out Gail's "spent" units from the right side instead. That made everything line up so much better.

Catherine was making bracelets using plastic beads. One-fourth of her beads were red, and she had 4 more blue beads than red beads. The remaining beads were yellow. If there were 32 beads in all, how many more yellow beads than red beads did Catherine have?

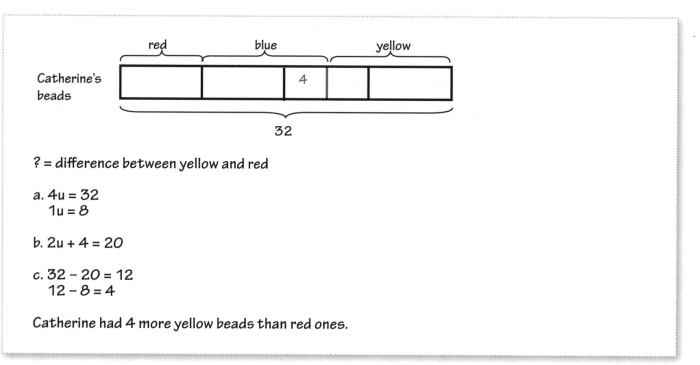

? = difference between yellow and red

a. 4u = 32
   1u = 8

b. 2u + 4 = 20

c. 32 – 20 = 12
   12 – 8 = 4

Catherine had 4 more yellow beads than red ones.

This is a part-whole problem. Part-whole problems fall into 2 categories. In one type you know something about the 2 or more parts, and you need to find the value of the whole; you do that by adding or multiplying. In the other type, you know the whole and some of the parts, and you need to find the value of the other part(s); you do that by subtracting or dividing.

That's about as simple as I can make this explanation, and it still sounds pretty wordy! When we recite rules and procedures to kids, it probably sounds pretty much like this. Doesn't a visual model like the one above give you a much clearer way to explain what you mean by a part-whole problem?

The challenge here is figuring out how to show the right proportions in the model. At the point when you're drawing the model, it's not clear how big to make the "4" space for the additional blue beads. Don't worry about it. The model may not be completely proportional, but it does the trick of showing how the parts relate to each other and to the whole.

You can also use this problem to get kids thinking a little bit more when placing the question mark. Every time you write a problem for your students, give that problem a little twist that goes beyond the scope of the previous problem. For example, the problem before this one might have asked, "How many yellow beads does Catherine have?" It would have been easy to figure out where to put the question mark for that. With this one, students need to recognize that there's no obvious place for the question mark within the model and that they just need to note the question below the drawing.

Fractions

If $\frac{3}{8}$ of a sum of money is \$384, what is $\frac{1}{4}$ of the money?

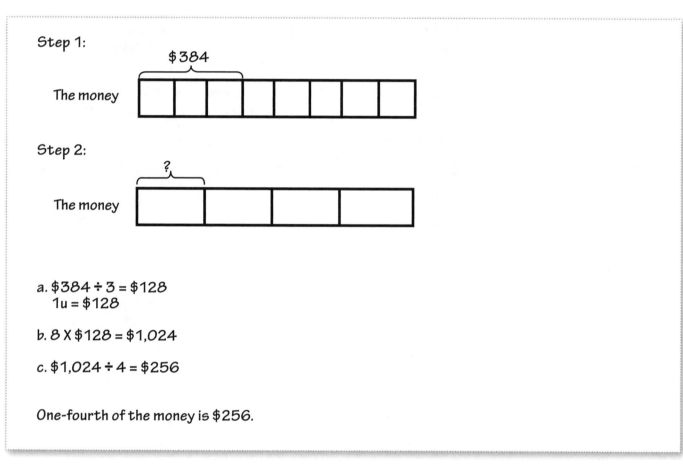

Step 1:

$384

The money

Step 2:

?

The money

a. \$384 ÷ 3 = \$128
   1u = \$128

b. 8 X \$128 = \$1,024

c. \$1,024 ÷ 4 = \$256

One-fourth of the money is \$256.

Ask yourself, "Is the sum of the money changing?" No, so make the bar in Step 2 the same length as the bar in Step 1. This time, though, divide the new bar into fourths.

I see problems like this all the time in algebra 1 textbooks. Model drawing makes them so easy to visualize and understand.

Another Way

Try adding a little color to show the different relationships within a single unit bar.

Look at the first bar model in this problem.

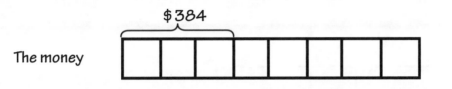

Ask your students if they see units that are equal to $\frac{1}{4}$ of the bar. When you drop in a little color, I bet they'll see them.

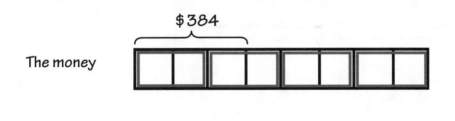

Now start the computation the same way you did in the 2-step model. Using this version, once you know that 1 black unit equals $128, you can finish the computation just by finding the value of 2 black units (the equivalent of 1 red unit).

When Erin and Amy went shopping, they started with a total of $91. Amy spent $25 and Erin spent $\frac{3}{5}$ of her money. At that point, Amy realized her remaining money was 3 times Erin's remaining money. How much money did Amy have when she started shopping?

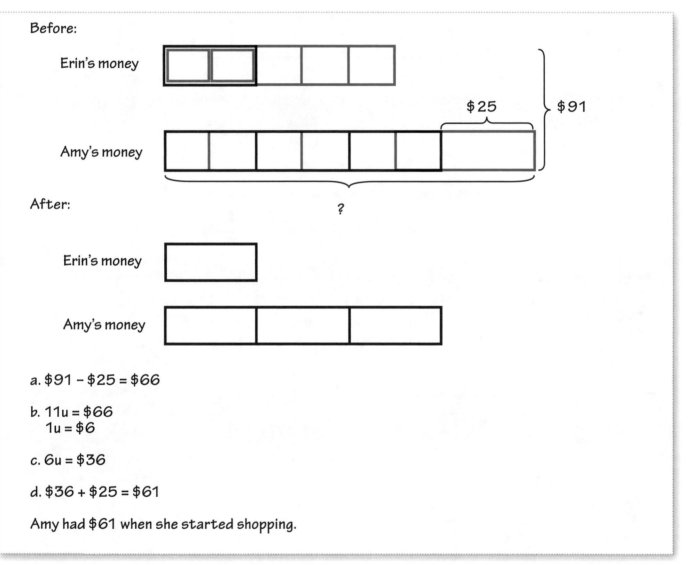

Before:

Erin's money

Amy's money

$25

$91

After:

?

Erin's money

Amy's money

a. $91 − $25 = $66

b. 11u = $66
   1u = $6

c. 6u = $36

d. $36 + $25 = $61

Amy had $61 when she started shopping.

For a lot of these before-and-after problems, it's easier to draw the "After" model first. Once you've done that, it's just a matter of adjusting that model, using the information in the problem, to discover what the "Before" model should look like.

The real trick here was figuring out how to adjust Erin's "Before" model. If she spent $\frac{3}{5}$ of her money, what fraction represents what she didn't spend? Right: $\frac{2}{5}$! So I needed to make that single black unit look like $\frac{2}{5}$ of a larger unit. To do that, I divided that black unit into 2 red units and added 3 more red units on the end.

Amy's "Before" was easy. I just needed to add a unit on the end and label it $25. (Don't make this unit the same size as the others.)

I call the next step subdividing the units. (That's my term—it's probably not something you'll find in another math book!) To give your students some background knowledge, show them this comparison.

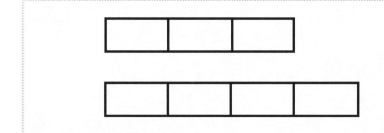

Ask them if you could use this model to show a comparison of 3 feet to 4 inches. Let's hope they say, "No." If they don't, you need to ask, "Which is greater: 3 feet or 4 inches?" Does the 3-unit to 4-unit model show that? No. Why? Because feet and inches are not the same unit of measure.

Kids need to really understand that you can't compare apples to oranges. If you want to compare 2 things, you must be using the same unit of measure for both. So to solve this problem, I had to make my unit size the same for both Amy and Erin. In this case I had already divided Erin's units in half, so I did the same thing to Amy's units. (These changes do not affect the comparison. It's like saying the ratio of 1 : 3 is the same as 2 : 6.)

The sum of Huan's and Jorge's ages is 60 years. Six years ago Huan's age was $\frac{1}{3}$ of Jorge's age. How old is each of them now?

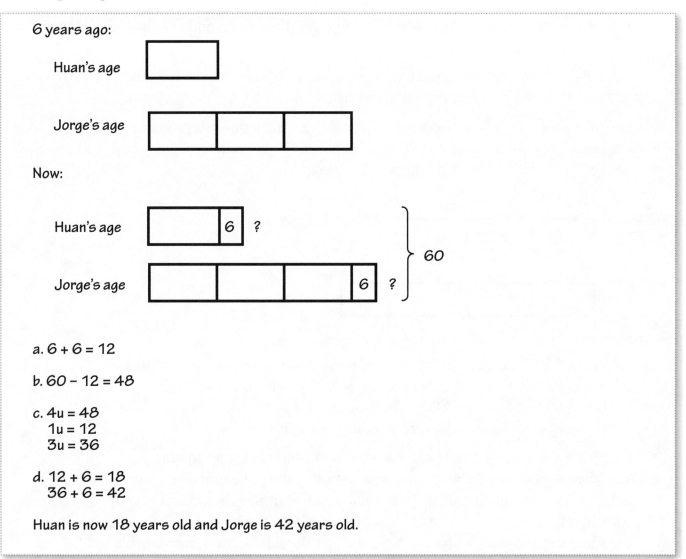

a. 6 + 6 = 12

b. 60 – 12 = 48

c. 4u = 48
   1u = 12
   3u = 36

d. 12 + 6 = 18
   36 + 6 = 42

Huan is now 18 years old and Jorge is 42 years old.

This problem is pretty straightforward as long as you start with Huan's and Jorge's ages 6 years ago. Some students may forget to do the final step in the computation (to arrive at their ages now), but putting the question marks in the appropriate places in the drawing should help them to avoid that possible error.

Sue and Sherry collect old postcards. After Sue sold $\frac{1}{5}$ of hers and Sherry sold 62 of hers, they each had the same number of postcards. If they started with 188 postcards altogether, how many did Sue end up with?

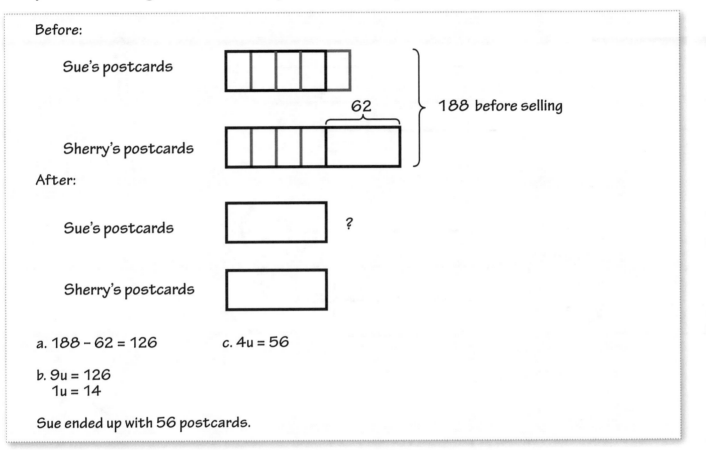

Before:

Sue's postcards

62   188 before selling

Sherry's postcards

After:

Sue's postcards   ?

Sherry's postcards

a. 188 − 62 = 126   c. 4u = 56

b. 9u = 126
   1u = 14

Sue ended up with 56 postcards.

Like many before-and-after problems, this problem is easier to solve if you start with the "After" drawing. That part is *really* easy: just make 2 equal bars.

Now for the "Before" drawing. My thinking was that since Sue sold $\frac{1}{5}$ of her original postcards, what she ended up with must be $\frac{4}{5}$ of the original amount. So I just copied her "After" bar, divided that unit into 4 equal parts, and tacked 1 more part on the end.

For Sherry's "Before" bar, I used a similar process. I copied her "After" bar and added another piece with a value of 62 to show Sherry's original amount. Then, since I know I always need to be comparing units of equal size, I divided the rest of her bar into 4 equal parts, making those parts the same size as Sue's.

Once you have things set up with equal-sized units, it becomes clear what computation you need to do.

Fractions

Grace had 16 more comic books than Mark. After Mark gave Grace 12 of his comic books, he realized he then had $\frac{1}{2}$ as many as Grace. How many comic books did Grace end up with?

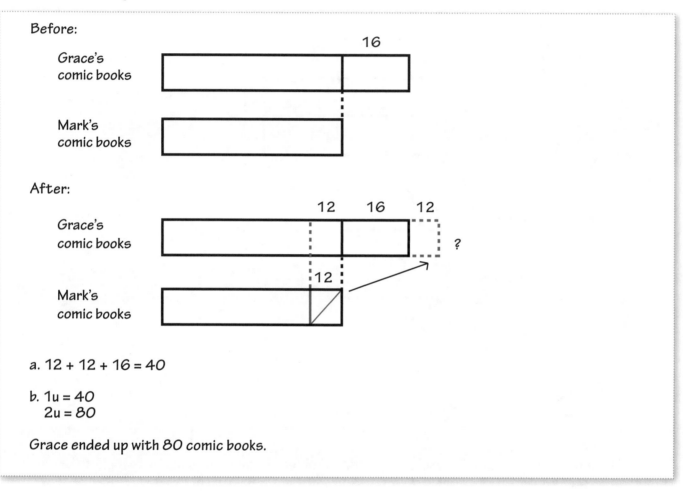

Before:

Grace's comic books

16

Mark's comic books

After:

Grace's comic books

12   16   12

?

Mark's comic books

12

a. 12 + 12 + 16 = 40

b. 1u = 40
   2u = 80

Grace ended up with 80 comic books.

The computation for this one is not complicated, so, as with many problems, the tricks are: 1) setting up the model correctly; and 2) using the model to figure out what computation you need to do. When the computation is quite basic, as in this problem, ask your students to do it mentally. Including mental math practice in daily computation is always a good idea.

When I'm solving a comparison problem in which one number is $\frac{1}{2}$ of a second number, I often turn things around. If Mark had $\frac{1}{2}$ as many as Grace, then Grace had twice as many as Mark. If kids are going to really understand math and solving word problems, they need to be comfortable with this type of conversion.

Decomposing numbers for easier computation or converting a number from one form to another is all part of understanding math. It's important to talk about these things and practice them a lot in your classroom.

One more tip: notice how I used the arrow to track the movement of a unit with a value of 12 from Mark's bar model to Grace's. In a comparison model, just adding that little arrow showing movement of some quantity may bring the model into 20/20 focus for a student.

Two-fifths of all the boys from Central School and $\frac{3}{4}$ of all the girls in the school attended the baseball game. If the number of boys at the game was the same as the number of girls, what fraction of the school's students attended the game?

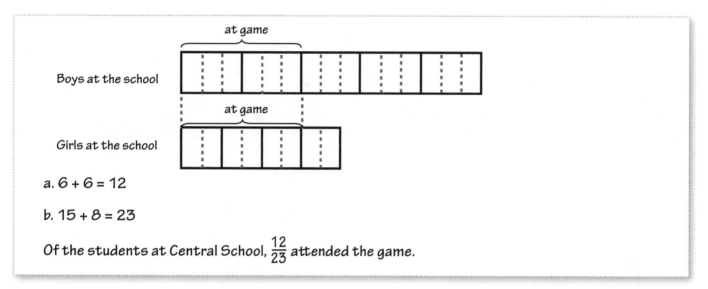

a. 6 + 6 = 12

b. 15 + 8 = 23

Of the students at Central School, $\frac{12}{23}$ attended the game.

Note that this is another example of a problem without a clear spot where the question mark should go in the model. In several earlier problems, I handled that by writing "? = . . ." below the model. An alternative approach is to write your answer as a statement and just put a blank where the final number answer will go. Then, of course, fill in that blank once you've solved the problem.

This problem is a bit different in that you don't do a lot of computation. Your answer is derived mostly from looking at the adjusted model. Pay close attention and you'll find that, as my friend Erik Latoni says, the model is talking to you.

Once you've manipulated the model to the stage at which you have 2 of the 5 boy units equaling 3 of the 4 girl units, you need to subdivide these different-sized units in order to compare them. I look at the 2 units and 3 units and think of the common multiple: 6.

If you divide the boy units into thirds and the girl units into halves, you now have a comparison of equal-sized units—15 boy units compared to 8 girl units. Remind your students that if you're going to compare things, you have to use the same unit of measure for each one. It's like comparing 4 yards to 6 feet. You have to change the 4 yards into the smaller unit of measure, feet, before you can do the comparison.

Now it's easy. The 15 units and 8 units represent all the students in the school, and the 6 boy units and 6 girl units represent students at the game.

23 Fractions

Marcia and Liz are quilters. Marcia had $\frac{3}{4}$ as many squares of fabric as Liz. After Liz took $\frac{3}{8}$ of her collection and sent it to Marcia, Marcia had 180 fabric squares. How many fabric squares did Liz end up with?

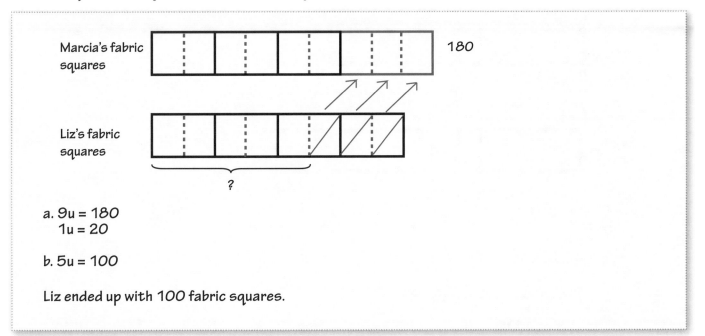

a. 9u = 180
   1u = 20

b. 5u = 100

Liz ended up with 100 fabric squares.

Because Liz's final collection is described in eighths, it makes sense to divide each of the original units in half. From there, the computation is pretty simple.

Another Way

Did you think about solving this as a before-and-after problem? You definitely could. The solution I provided above just happens to be the path my brain took on this problem. My friend and colleague Char Forsten has a favorite acronym: WOW! It stands for Whichever One Works! I might adjust that slightly and say, "WOWY!" (Whichever One Works for You). Isn't it great that we don't all have to use exactly the same procedure to reach the same answer?

Karen's money was $\frac{5}{6}$ of Kay's. After Kay saved another $30, Karen's money was only $\frac{2}{3}$ of Kay's. In the end, how much more money did Kay have than Karen?

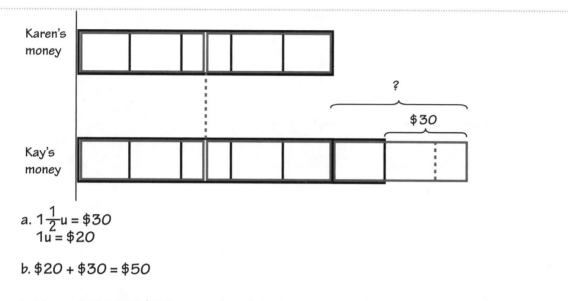

a. $1\frac{1}{2}$u = $30
   1u = $20

b. $20 + $30 = $50

In the end, Kay had $50 more than Karen.

I find using colored pencils really helps me when I need to adjust the model.

For this problem, I started out by drawing 5 units for Karen and 6 for Kay. That showed the first sentence of the problem.

Next I needed to show that Karen's 5 units are now $\frac{2}{3}$ of Kay's units. That's the same as saying the ratio of Karen's units to Kay's is 2 : 3. So I used the colored pencil to group Karen's original 5 units into 2 larger red units, and I grouped Kay's units the same way. It then became clear that the solid red unit on the right of Kay's bar (or, for that matter, any of the red units) was equal to $2\frac{1}{2}$ of the original black units—and it was easy to see how to handle the computation.

Another thing that sometimes helps is a ruler. Though I usually draw these models free-hand, there are times with the more complicated problems when I can visualize the relationships better if I try to draw more exactly and line things up with vertical rules. Some folks like to use graph paper, and some work with lined paper positioned horizontally. If you have kids who are just learning to use model drawing, you might suggest they always begin their comparison-model solutions with a starting line on the left as I've done here.

Another Way

An alternative approach would be to divide all the larger units in half, like this.

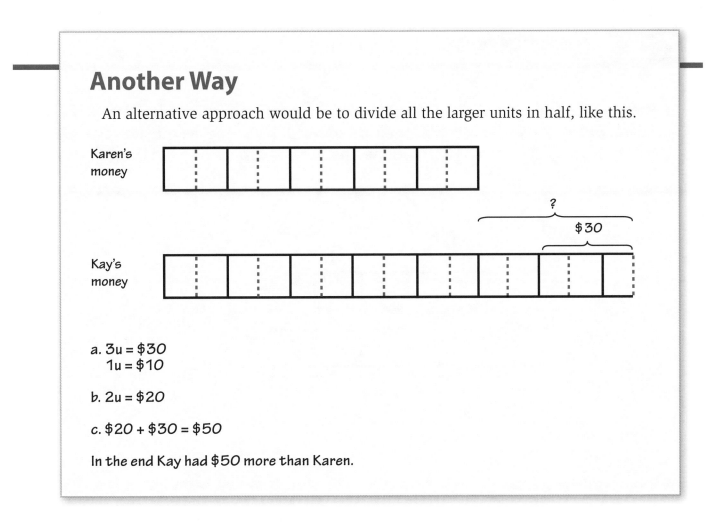

Karen's money

Kay's money

?

$30

a. 3u = $30
   1u = $10

b. 2u = $20

c. $20 + $30 = $50

In the end Kay had $50 more than Karen.

Patty earned an extra $35 on Monday and an extra $16 on Tuesday. After that, her friend Betsey had $\frac{2}{5}$ as much as their neighbor Jerry and $\frac{1}{3}$ as much as Patty. If the 3 of them together had $162.76 in the end, how much money did Patty start with?

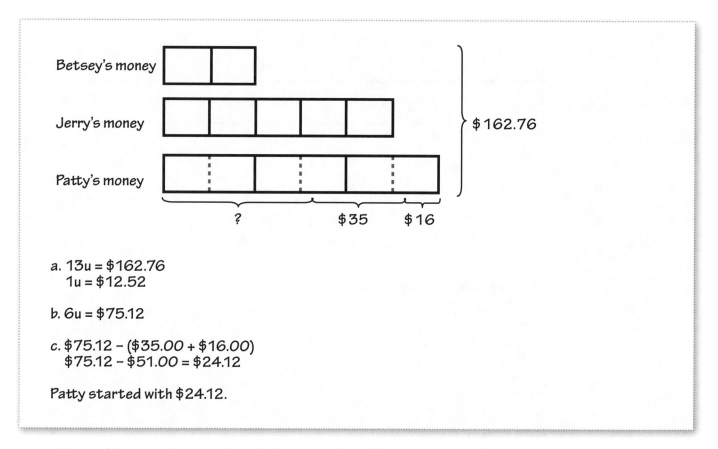

a. 13u = $162.76
   1u = $12.52

b. 6u = $75.12

c. $75.12 – ($35.00 + $16.00)
   $75.12 – $51.00 = $24.12

Patty started with $24.12.

Lots of times, when you're solving a word problem, you take the numbers in the order they appear in the problem, and you place them immediately in the model. This problem is a good example of how sometimes that *doesn't* work. In this case, it's easier to start with the comparison information that's given in the second sentence.

The part that's not so easy is the placement of the question mark on Patty's unit bar. At the stage when you're drawing the model, you have no idea how many units equal $16 or $35. But you do know that what's left will be the amount you're looking for—which means that's where your question mark needs to go. I'd suggest drawing the braces for the $16 and $35 so that they don't line up with an exact number of units in the bar model.

One-quarter of Elijah's marbles is equal to $\frac{2}{3}$ of Shelley's marbles. If Elijah has 35 more marbles than Shelley, how many marbles do they have altogether?

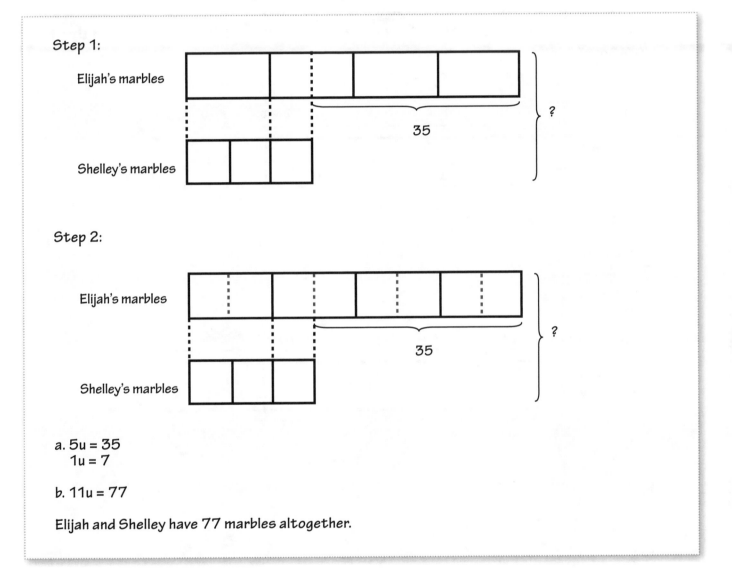

Step 1:

Elijah's marbles

Shelley's marbles

35

?

Step 2:

Elijah's marbles

Shelley's marbles

35

?

a. 5u = 35
   1u = 7

b. 11u = 77

Elijah and Shelley have 77 marbles altogether.

Before you can start computing, you know that the equal parts of Elijah's and Shelley's bar models need units that are the same size. This problem becomes very manageable once you divide each of Elijah's units in half.

Peg was making punch for the staff reception. As she filled the container, she realized that 6 bottles of cranberry juice took up $\frac{4}{7}$ of the container. The rest of the container was filled with 2 bottles plus 10 cups of lemonade. If the bottles of cranberry juice and lemonade were the same size, how many cups did the container hold?

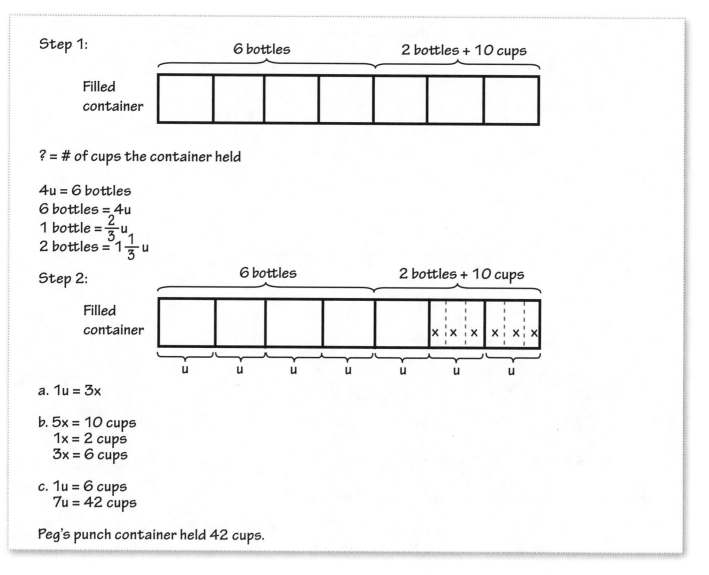

Step 1:

Filled container

6 bottles   2 bottles + 10 cups

? = # of cups the container held

$4u = 6$ bottles
6 bottles $= 4u$
1 bottle $= \frac{2}{3}u$
2 bottles $= 1\frac{1}{3}u$

Step 2:

Filled container

6 bottles   2 bottles + 10 cups

u   u   u   u   u   u   u

a. $1u = 3x$

b. $5x = 10$ cups
   $1x = 2$ cups
   $3x = 6$ cups

c. $1u = 6$ cups
   $7u = 42$ cups

Peg's punch container held 42 cups.

In Singapore, teachers say they don't reteach concepts, but they practice them often. This problem gives you a chance to practice properties of numbers.

When I'm solving a word problem, I usually start my computation with something like "4u = some amount." I started that way here, but as I was working the first part of the computation, I decided that what I really wanted to know was how 1 bottle would be described in terms of units. (I realize this step is not absolutely necessary, but it's like always having to put my right sock on first—it just works better for me.) I needed to reverse the equation. As you're working this step out with your students, don't forget to ask them what property of numbers allows this move. (It's the symmetric property.)

In Step 2 I needed to subdivide the last "u" units into thirds. I also needed to make a distinction between the "u" units and the smaller ones, so I decided to label each of the smaller units "x." Taking a little extra care with this labeling makes it easier to get to the finish.

This final computation gives you an opportunity to mention another number property—specifically, the transition property. That property allows us to say that if 1u = 3x and 3x = 6 cups, then 1u = 6 cups. Once you know that, it's easy to finish the calculation and answer the question.

Winandus spent $\frac{4}{5}$ of his money on 3 pillows and 4 vases. Each pillow cost twice as much as each vase. If he had $35 left after his shopping spree, how much did Winandus pay for each vase?

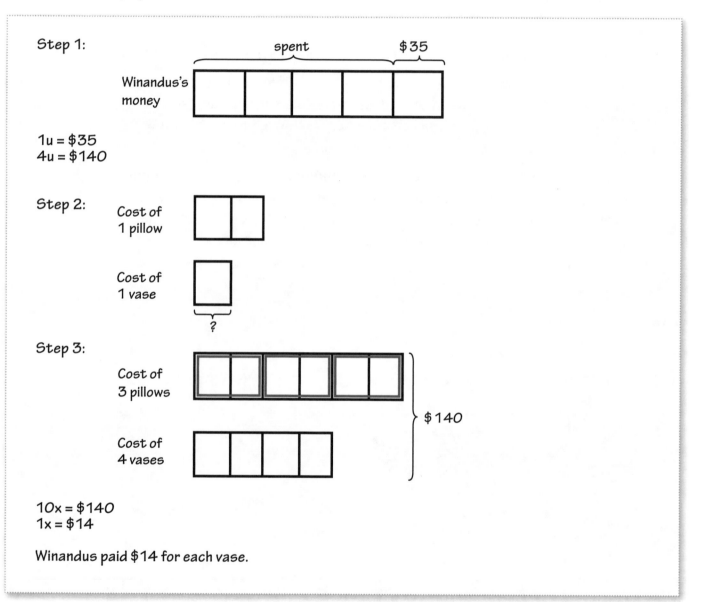

Step 1:

spent $35

Winandus's money

1u = $35
4u = $140

Step 2:

Cost of 1 pillow

Cost of 1 vase

?

Step 3:

Cost of 3 pillows

$140

Cost of 4 vases

10x = $140
1x = $14

Winandus paid $14 for each vase.

Don't be afraid to break a problem down into multiple steps and models. After I drew the bar model in Step 1, I wasn't sure how I was going to work the rest of the information in the problem into that model. Breaking the modeling and computation down into 3 separate steps took care of that and made things much clearer.

Together, tanks A and B hold 348 gallons. After a leak causes Tank A to lose $\frac{1}{5}$ of its liquid and someone removes 60 gallons from Tank B, the volume of the 2 tanks is equal. How much does each tank hold?

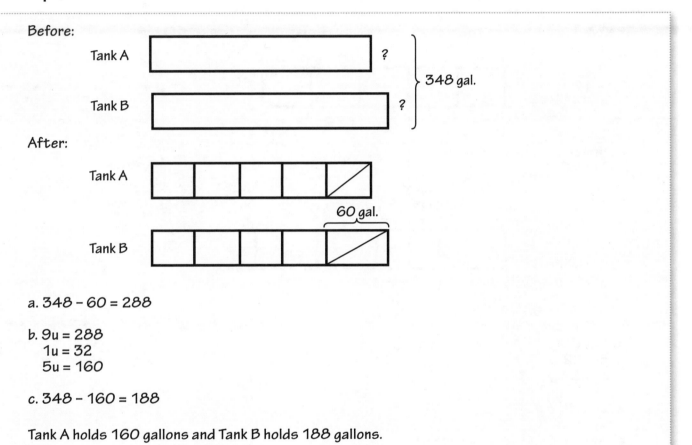

Before:

Tank A   ?

Tank B   ?   } 348 gal.

After:

Tank A

     60 gal.

Tank B

a. 348 − 60 = 288

b. 9u = 288
   1u = 32
   5u = 160

c. 348 − 160 = 188

Tank A holds 160 gallons and Tank B holds 188 gallons.

When you start to draw this model, consider:

- Are these tanks equal in size?

- Which tank is bigger?

You can't assume the tanks are the same size. Which is bigger? I wasn't sure when I started drawing.

Sometimes when I'm trying to figure out how to solve a problem, I ask myself questions like these. Then, even if I'm not sure of the exact way to go, I start drawing the model. When I discover I've got a glitch, I just adjust the drawing.

Encourage your students to take some risks and, when they're not sure how to approach a problem, to write down *something*. They can always erase!

The ConVal Drama Club had 40 members. Of those, $\frac{2}{5}$ were females. After an open audition, 20 new members joined the club, but the females still made up $\frac{2}{5}$ of the membership. How many new members were females?

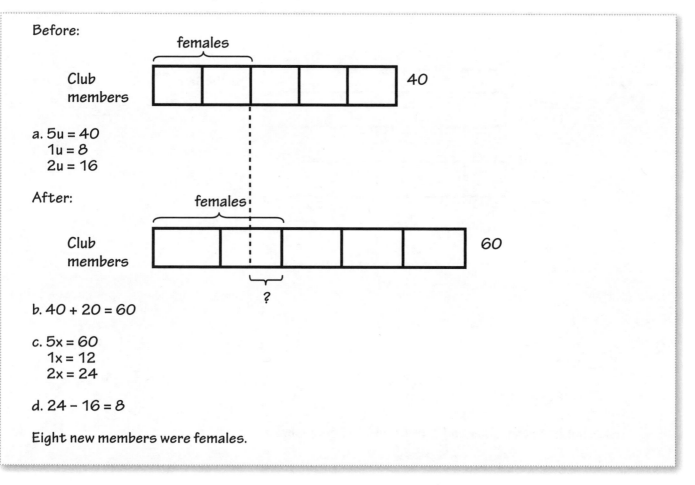

Before:

females

Club members   40

a. 5u = 40
   1u = 8
   2u = 16

After:

females

Club members   60

?

b. 40 + 20 = 60

c. 5x = 60
   1x = 12
   2x = 24

d. 24 – 16 = 8

Eight new members were females.

Wow! Is this problem implying that $\frac{2}{5}$ doesn't always equal $\frac{2}{5}$? Well, sort of.

Introducing a problem like this opens up opportunities for some great classroom discussions. We could all take a lesson (literally) from my teaching hero, Dr. Yeap Ban Har.

When Ban Har models problem solving with students in both Singapore and the United States, he plays the role of someone who doesn't understand how something like this could make sense. Then, by directing the right questions to his students, he gets them to figure out and explain the answer. Getting kids to communicate their thinking is a key to building math comprehension.

Following Ban Har's approach, let's use this problem to develop a deeper understanding of fractions. You might ask:

- *Is it clear from reading the problem whether the new members include both males and females?* No.

- *If $\frac{2}{5}$ of one number is equal to $\frac{2}{5}$ of another number, must those 2 numbers be the same?* Yes. (Test this on some examples to illustrate your point.)

- *What if you take $\frac{2}{5}$ of a smaller number and compare it to $\frac{2}{5}$ of a larger number? Do you get the same amount?* No.

Answering these questions and others like them requires a strong conceptual understanding of fractions—and if students are stumped by these questions initially, they'll develop that understanding as they figure out the answers.

That's not all you can do with this problem. After you've completed the computation together, you might also ask:

- *How could this problem be rewritten (without changing the meaning) so that it contains no fractions?* (If they get stuck, throw them a bone by saying, "percent," "ratio," or maybe "decimals." Challenge them to see how many ways they can rewrite the original problem.)

- *What was the original ratio of females to males?* (I'll bet you dollars-to-doughnuts someone will answer, "2 : 5," but not you! You know it's 2 : 3.)

Another Way

Some budding mathematician in your class may suggest that if the females still represented $\frac{2}{5}$ of the members even after the new people arrived, then $\frac{2}{5}$ of those new members must be females. That person is simply going to find $\frac{2}{5}$ of 20, and of course she'll arrive at the same answer: 8. I love to see a student who thinks differently than I do.

PROBLEM 31

Lorie spent $\frac{3}{5}$ of her money on gifts for Luann and Joan. Luann's gift cost 3 times as much as Joan's gift. If Lorie had $12 left after she made her purchases, how much did Luann's gift cost?

PROBLEM 32

The sum of 2 numbers is 10. The difference between the 2 numbers is $\frac{1}{3}$ of the greater number. What are the numbers?

PROBLEM 33

Ted and Barbara had the same amount of money. Ted gave $\frac{1}{3}$ of his to Tillie and Barbara gave $\frac{1}{4}$ of hers to Maddy. In the end Ted had $8 less than Barbara. How much did Ted and Barbara each have originally?

PROBLEM 34

Michele had 3 times as many cookies as Sally. Michele got really hungry in the afternoon and ate 20 of her cookies. Afterward Michele had only $\frac{1}{2}$ as many cookies as Sally. How many cookies did Sally have?

PROBLEM 35

Ebby had a job mowing lawns. After 3 days she still had $\frac{5}{7}$ of the lawns left to mow. In the next 3 days she increased her speed and mowed $1\frac{1}{2}$ times as many as in the first 3 days, but she still had 6 more lawns to mow. How many lawns did she have to mow in total?

Ed decided to buy lobsters for the family. He paid $8.60 per pound for small lobsters and $7.50 per pound for larger lobsters. At the checkout counter he handed the clerk a $100 bill and got $0.70 back in change. He remembered hearing the clerk say there were 5.5 pounds of the larger lobsters. How many pounds of the smaller lobsters did Ed buy?

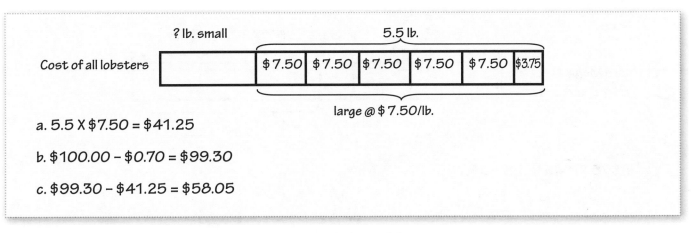

a. 5.5 X $7.50 = $41.25

b. $100.00 – $0.70 = $99.30

c. $99.30 – $41.25 = $58.05

At this point this turns into a basic part-whole problem.

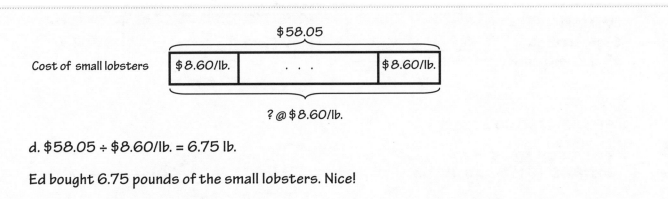

d. $58.05 ÷ $8.60/lb. = 6.75 lb.

Ed bought 6.75 pounds of the small lobsters. Nice!

When I looked at the initial model, I asked myself what else I knew that could help me answer the question. Was the model telling me anything? The answer was yes. I could figure out how much money Ed spent on the large lobsters.

Then I realized I hadn't used the information about the $100 bill that was included in the problem. That amount less the change would give me the total spent.

Once I got that far, I was on a roll, and I could see the rest of the computation I needed to do.

During the month of February, Lil put purchases of $75.20 and $18.35 on her Mega Store charge account, and the store charged her $8.32 in interest. Lil also made a payment of $90. Her next bill showed a balance of $206.40. What was her balance prior to February?

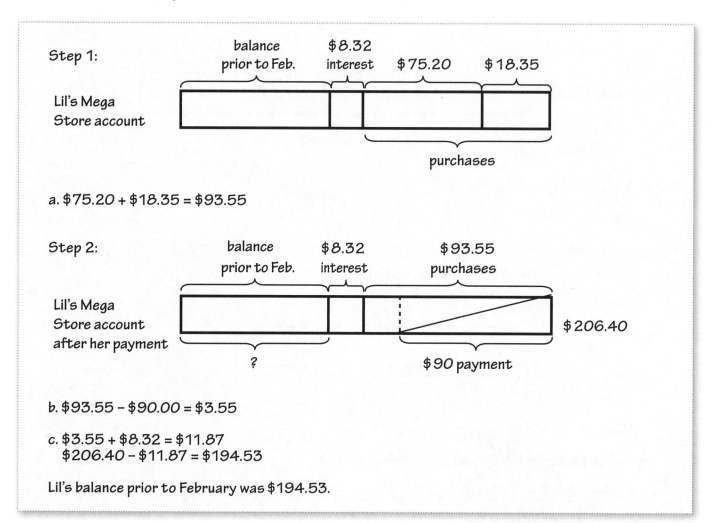

Step 1:

balance prior to Feb. $8.32 interest $75.20 $18.35

Lil's Mega Store account

purchases

a. $75.20 + $18.35 = $93.55

Step 2:

balance prior to Feb. $8.32 interest $93.55 purchases

Lil's Mega Store account after her payment

? $90 payment $206.40

b. $93.55 – $90.00 = $3.55

c. $3.55 + $8.32 = $11.87
   $206.40 – $11.87 = $194.53

Lil's balance prior to February was $194.53.

This is a pretty wordy problem. I can just see my students' eyes glazing over after reading one like this. But that's why model drawing is so great. It takes a "NWISTO" problem, adds a visual, and makes it easy to solve. ("NWISTO" is student code for "No Way—I'm Skipping This One!")

I can't stress enough that one of the great things about using this method of problem solving is that there isn't always just one correct way to set things up. Celebrate when you and your students come up with alternative models or methods of computation—but always remember to ask the students to explain their thinking. You want to look inside their heads and find out the thought process behind that great idea.

38 Decimals

When Stacy babysat for Lucy and Owen, she was paid $10 per hour for any time up to 10:00 p.m. and $8 per hour for any time after 10:00 p.m. When the parents got home, they paid Stacy $98, which included a $5 tip. If Stacy started sitting at 3:30 p.m., when did the parents get home?

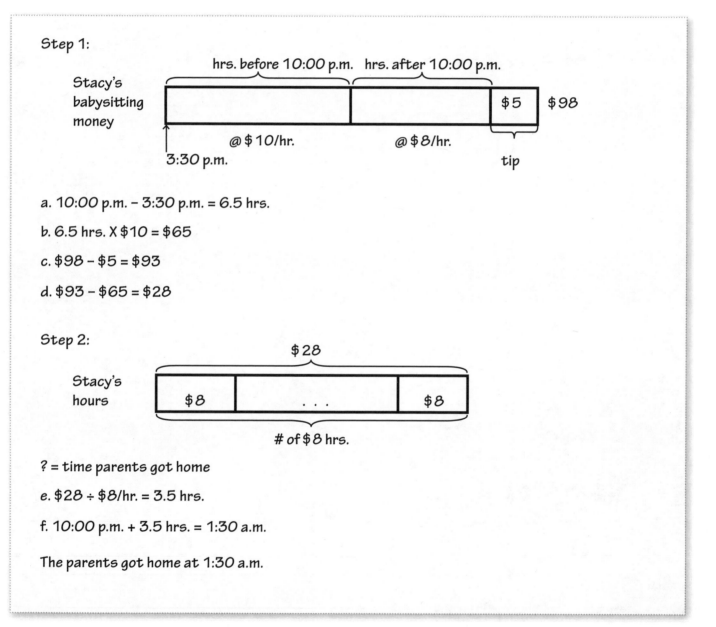

Step 1:

a. 10:00 p.m. – 3:30 p.m. = 6.5 hrs.

b. 6.5 hrs. X $10 = $65

c. $98 – $5 = $93

d. $93 – $65 = $28

Step 2:

? = time parents got home

e. $28 ÷ $8/hr. = 3.5 hrs.

f. 10:00 p.m. + 3.5 hrs. = 1:30 a.m.

The parents got home at 1:30 a.m.

Even though this problem is really just a part-whole problem, it has a lot of little extras—like calculating elapsed time—to consider. The trick is to avoid getting overwhelmed. Just take it one step at a time.

It's not essential to show the additional part-whole model to find the number of $8 hours, but it doesn't do any harm reminding your students what division really looks like. A lot of kids know that multiplication is the same as repeated addition, but some of them miss the point that division is the same as repeated subtraction.

Another Way

You could also show the last step using repeated subtraction—like this:

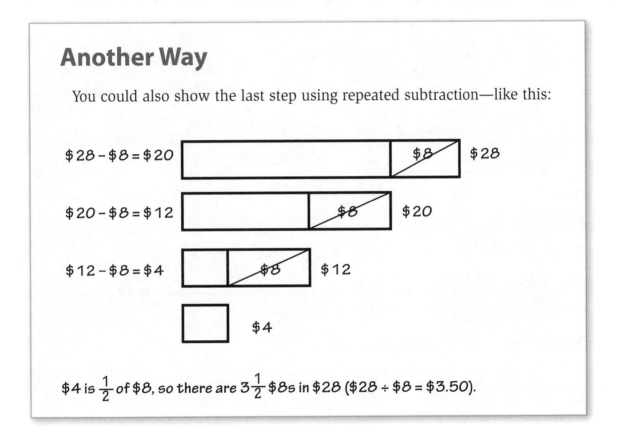

$4 is $\frac{1}{2}$ of $8, so there are $3\frac{1}{2}$ $8s in $28 ($28 ÷ $8 = $3.50).

At the end of the week, Ashley checked her wallet and saw she had $36.42. She recalled that on Thursday, Linda had given her $5 for a book, but that later that same day Jeremy had borrowed $3 for a latté. She also remembered that at the start of the week, she had given her husband half of the money she had at that time. How much money did Ashley have at the beginning of the week?

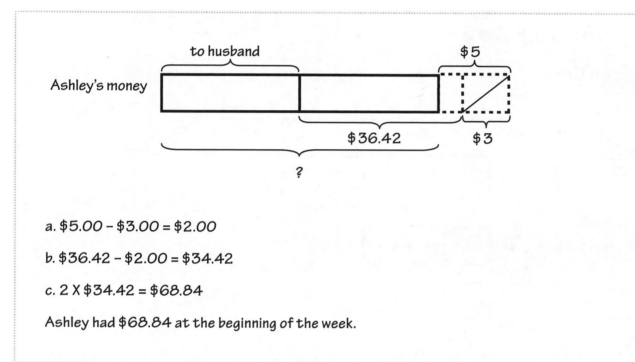

a. $5.00 – $3.00 = $2.00

b. $36.42 – $2.00 = $34.42

c. 2 X $34.42 = $68.84

Ashley had $68.84 at the beginning of the week.

Probably the trickiest part of this problem is reading carefully enough to real-ize that the money exchange Ashley had with Linda and Jeremy happened *after* Ashley had divided her money to give half to her husband. It's actually easier to draw the model as it would appear at the beginning of the week and then add on the other exchanges of money that took place later.

Originally, Anni had $\frac{2}{3}$ as much money as Jana, but then Jana gave $\frac{1}{2}$ of her money to Anni as a birthday present. Anni also got a $25 check as a gift from her friend Sandy. If Anni ended up with $77.50, how much money did she have originally?

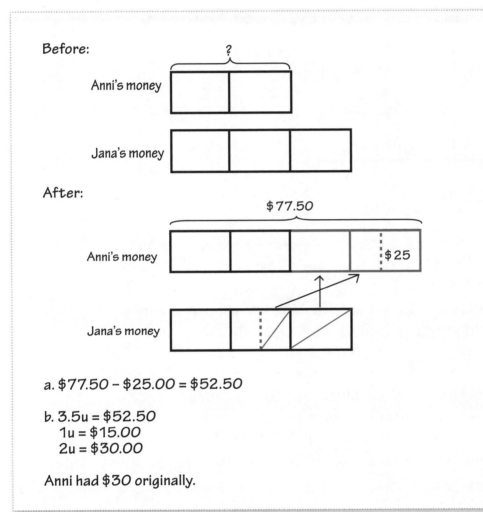

a. $77.50 – $25.00 = $52.50

b. 3.5u = $52.50
   1u = $15.00
   2u = $30.00

Anni had $30 originally.

   This solution keeps the units in the "After" model the same size as the ones in the "Before" model. I moved 1.5 units from Jana's unit bar to Anni's, and then added on another piece (not necessarily the same size) to represent the $25 gift from Sandy.

   The piece showing Sandy's gift turns out to be disproportionate; sometimes after you arrive at a solution, you realize that your model isn't proportionately accurate. You may decide that's okay, or you may want to adjust your model at the end. But when you're setting up a model, you have to work with what you know at the time.

Another Way

An alternative would be to divide each of the original units (except the $25 one) in half, like this:

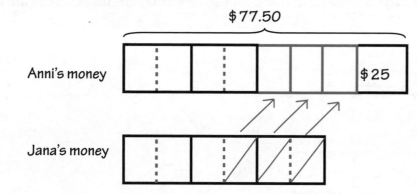

$77.50

Anni's money

$25

Jana's money

a. $77.50 – $25.00 = $52.50

b. 7u = $52.50
1u = $7.50
4u = $30.00

A good follow-up question for this problem would be, "What portion of Sandy's money did she give to Anni?" We don't really know, do we? I can assure you that some students are going to want to put Sandy in the drawing, and they'll probably be a little frustrated that they don't know how to describe the money Sandy didn't give away. We'll just never know how generous Sandy was. Maybe she was very generous because she only had a total of $30, or maybe she's a secret millionaire and could have easily given more. Oh, the mystery of it all.

PROBLEM 41

At the beginning of the week, the difference between Ricardo's money and Liliana's money was $12.50. By the end of the week they had each spent half of their money, and they had a total of $137.85 left. How much did each of them start with? Who had the most money?

PROBLEM 42

Matt has 0.75 times as much money as Todd and Todd has 0.8 times as much as Katie. If Katie has $128.80, how much do they have altogether?

PROBLEM 43

Samantha was making bags for a crafts fair. She bought 12 yards of fabric at $9.79 per yard for the outside of the bags, and she bought 9 yards of fabric at $6.95 per yard to use for the bag linings. She sold all the finished bags for a total of $318.78. What was her profit?

PROBLEM 44

Shernece decided everyone on her holiday shopping list would get a hat or a scarf. The hats cost $18.95 each, and the scarves cost $28.95 each; she purchased 5 more hats than scarves. If her total purchases came to $477.95, how many hats did she buy?

Rate/Distance

A car and a truck were traveling on the same road from Town A to Town B. The towns were 540 miles apart. The truck traveled at an average rate of 60 miles per hour. The car left Town A an hour after the truck, and it arrived at Town B $\frac{1}{2}$ hour before the truck. What was the average speed of the car?

Sometimes the visual you use doesn't look like the typical bar model drawing. Usually a line (or multiple lines) works better for distance problems. I tell kids the road between the 2 towns probably looks more like this:

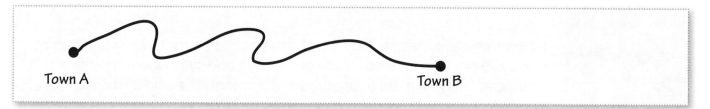

But for ease of drawing and visualizing, I'm going to imagine the road stretched out nice and straight.

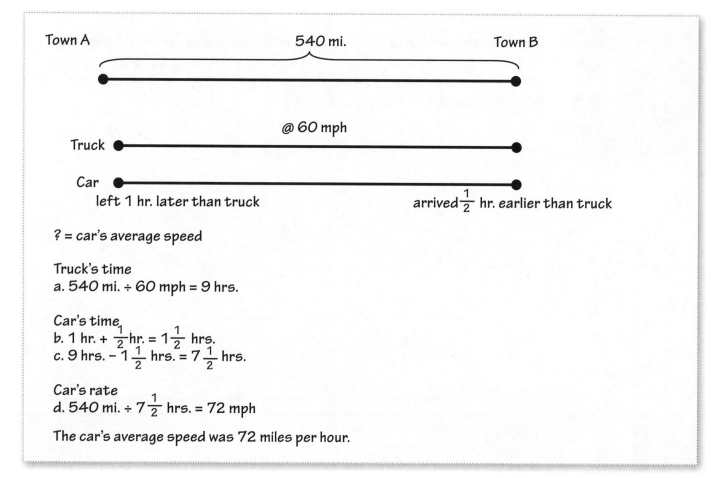

? = car's average speed

Truck's time
a. 540 mi. ÷ 60 mph = 9 hrs.

Car's time
b. 1 hr. + $\frac{1}{2}$ hr. = $1\frac{1}{2}$ hrs.
c. 9 hrs. − $1\frac{1}{2}$ hrs. = $7\frac{1}{2}$ hrs.

Car's rate
d. 540 mi. ÷ $7\frac{1}{2}$ hrs. = 72 mph

The car's average speed was 72 miles per hour.

When you start solving this problem, it's a good idea to have a discussion with your students about the travel time of both the truck and the car. After reading through the problem together, ask them, "Which was on the road longer, the car or the truck?" Don't get into details of *how much* longer the truck was on the road; just try to get them to see the big picture first. You might want them to consider what the model would look like if you drew it to show time rather than distance.

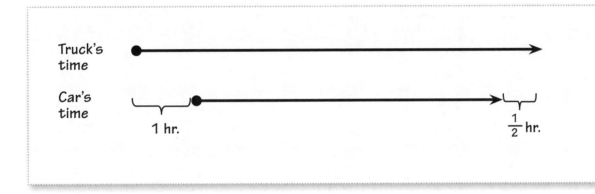

Ask students to think about how the car, which left after the truck, still managed to beat the truck to the destination. Can they explain their reasoning? Get them thinking about the inverse relationship of time and speed before they actually start the computation work. You want them to verbalize the fact that the vehicle that was on the road for the shorter amount of time must have been traveling faster. Then, instead of just doing the computation, they'll be able to recognize whether their answer makes sense.

On Tia's trip to New Hampshire, her average rate of speed for the whole 5-hour trip was 62 miles per hour. For the first 2 hours of her trip, she kept her average speed at 50 miles per hour. Then she realized she was going to be late for her appointment, so she started driving faster. What was her average speed for the last 3 hours of her trip?

Step 1:

? mi.

Tia's 5-hr. trip

62 mph	62 mph	62 mph	62 mph	62 mph

a. 5 hrs. X 62 mph = 310 mi.

Step 2:

310 mi.

Tia's 5-hr. trip

50 mph	50 mph	?		

b. 2 X 50 mi. = 100 mi.

c. 310 mi. – 100 mi. = 210 mi.

d. 210 mi. ÷ 3 hrs. = 70 mph

Tia's average speed for the last 3 hours of her trip was 70 miles per hour.

Speed (or distance/rate/time) problems like this one are easy to visualize using the part-whole model. Here I'm letting the whole be the distance; the 5 parts represent the 5 hours Tia traveled. Within each unit I'm indicating her average speed for that hour.

The initial model illustrates the fact that the average speed for all 5 hours was 62 miles per hour. From that I can calculate the total distance traveled and can move to Step 2 to find the average for the last 3 hours.

It looks like Tia has a bit of a lead foot!

Rate/Distance

Ellen and Holly took a road trip together. Ellen drove at an average of 45 miles per hour for the first $\frac{3}{7}$ of the total distance, and Holly drove the last 24 miles at an average rate of 54 miles per hour. How long did the trip take the 2 of them? Give your answer in terms of hours.

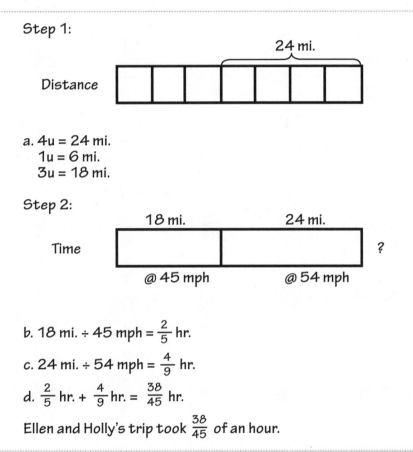

Step 1:

24 mi.

Distance

a. 4u = 24 mi.
   1u = 6 mi.
   3u = 18 mi.

Step 2:

18 mi.   24 mi.

Time   ?

@ 45 mph   @ 54 mph

b. 18 mi. ÷ 45 mph = $\frac{2}{5}$ hr.

c. 24 mi. ÷ 54 mph = $\frac{4}{9}$ hr.

d. $\frac{2}{5}$ hr. + $\frac{4}{9}$ hr. = $\frac{38}{45}$ hr.

Ellen and Holly's trip took $\frac{38}{45}$ of an hour.

You know that to find time, you want to apply the formula T = D ÷ R. But this problem involves 2 different rates, so first you need to figure the distance each person traveled. That's Step 1.

When you get to Step 2, figuring the time, it's important to check what unit of measure the problem is asking you to use. Of course, if you want to give your students an extra challenge, you can ask them to convert the answer to minutes, rounding to the nearest minute. (They should say 51 minutes.)

I think it's a good idea to cover problems like this one—problems that have what some students might think of as "weird" answers—occasionally. I found my students thinking correct answers would always work out to be nice, common fractions like $\frac{2}{3}$, $\frac{3}{4}$, $\frac{1}{5}$, and so on. I remember a time when a girl who was taking a quiz asked if there was something wrong with a problem because the answer looked so "weird." In real life those "weird" answers come up, so getting kids used to that is a good thing.

Janet and David took a trip together to visit their father. When they arrived, their father asked them how long the trip had taken. Janet said that she had driven the first 450 miles, which represented $\frac{3}{7}$ of the total distance, and David had driven the rest. David said the average speed for the whole trip was 45 miles per hour. If they stopped for 30 minutes to eat lunch, what was the answer to their father's question? (Include the lunch time in their total travel time.)

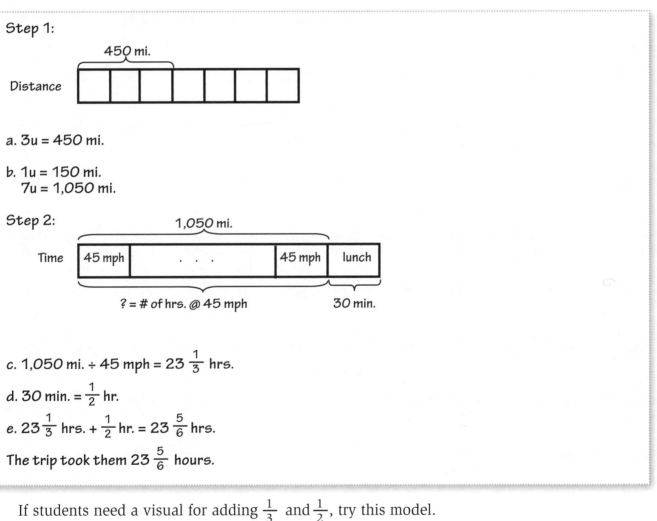

Step 1:

450 mi.

Distance

a. 3u = 450 mi.

b. 1u = 150 mi.
7u = 1,050 mi.

Step 2:

1,050 mi.

Time | 45 mph | . . . | 45 mph | lunch

? = # of hrs. @ 45 mph   30 min.

c. 1,050 mi. ÷ 45 mph = 23 $\frac{1}{3}$ hrs.

d. 30 min. = $\frac{1}{2}$ hr.

e. 23 $\frac{1}{3}$ hrs. + $\frac{1}{2}$ hr. = 23 $\frac{5}{6}$ hrs.

The trip took them 23 $\frac{5}{6}$ hours.

If students need a visual for adding $\frac{1}{3}$ and $\frac{1}{2}$, try this model.

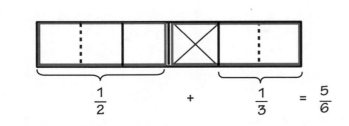

$$\frac{1}{2} \quad + \quad \frac{1}{3} \quad = \quad \frac{5}{6}$$

You can kick this problem up a notch by asking students to express their answer in hours and minutes. Or, better still, tell them what time Janet and David arrived at their father's house and ask them at what time they started their trip.

Bill and Dorothy left Phoenix, traveling north to a dance contest in Taptown. Dorothy drove $\frac{1}{4}$ of the distance at an average rate of 50 miles per hour. The couple then took 45 minutes for lunch. When they started up again, Bill drove for the remaining 225 miles. If their average speed for the entire trip was 60 miles per hour, what was Bill's average speed?

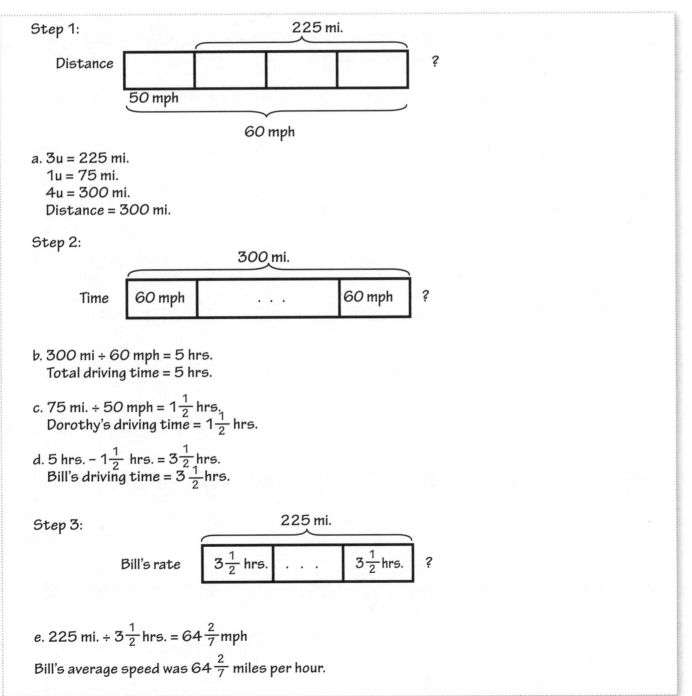

Step 1:

225 mi.

Distance

50 mph

60 mph

?

a. 3u = 225 mi.
   1u = 75 mi.
   4u = 300 mi.
   Distance = 300 mi.

Step 2:

300 mi.

Time | 60 mph | . . . | 60 mph | ?

b. 300 mi. ÷ 60 mph = 5 hrs.
   Total driving time = 5 hrs.

c. 75 mi. ÷ 50 mph = $1\frac{1}{2}$ hrs.
   Dorothy's driving time = $1\frac{1}{2}$ hrs.

d. 5 hrs. − $1\frac{1}{2}$ hrs. = $3\frac{1}{2}$ hrs.
   Bill's driving time = $3\frac{1}{2}$ hrs.

Step 3:

225 mi.

Bill's rate | $3\frac{1}{2}$ hrs. | . . . | $3\frac{1}{2}$ hrs. | ?

e. 225 mi. ÷ $3\frac{1}{2}$ hrs. = $64\frac{2}{7}$ mph

Bill's average speed was $64\frac{2}{7}$ miles per hour.

This appears to be a very complicated problem, but once you break it down into the 3 separate components of a DRT problem, it's manageable. Always look at what you're trying to find—in this case one of the rates. To do that, you need to first find the distance and then find the time.

Did you notice that this problem had some additional information that had no effect on the solution? Did it matter that they were heading north? No. Did you need the amount of time they spent eating lunch? No. Students need to see that sometimes they don't have to use every bit of the information given.

PROBLEM 50

Mark and Liz entered a scooter race of 72 miles. Mark arrived late and started the race 30 minutes later than Liz, but he whizzed down the road at 18 miles per hour. If they finished the race at the same time, what was Liz's average speed?

PROBLEM 51

Fernando and Ron each drove from Peterborough to Honesdale. They started at the same time, and each traveled at a uniform speed. When Fernando reached Honesdale, Ron was still 78 miles away. Ron reached Honesdale $1\frac{1}{2}$ hours after Fernando got there. If the 2 towns are 390 miles apart, at what speed was Fernando traveling?

PROBLEM 52

Finn and Ella started traveling at the same time, from the same spot, but in opposite directions. After 2 hours they were 176 miles apart. If Finn's average speed was 2 miles per hour faster than Ella's, what was Ella's average speed?

Cheryl had $\frac{1}{12}$ as many books as Brenda. Later Cheryl bought 18 more books. If Brenda has 72 books, what will be the ratio of Cheryl's books to Brenda's after Cheryl's purchase?

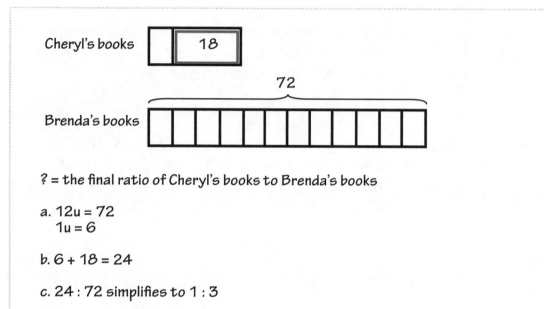

? = the final ratio of Cheryl's books to Brenda's books

a. 12u = 72
   1u = 6

b. 6 + 18 = 24

c. 24 : 72 simplifies to 1 : 3

The ratio of Cheryl's books to Brenda's books will be 1 : 3.

When you begin planning the model for this problem, first think about the big picture. Think about questions like these:

- *Who has fewer books to start?* Cheryl.

- *Is Cheryl's unit bar going to get bigger or smaller?* Bigger.

- *How is Brenda's unit bar changing?* It's not changing.

After you've mentally visualized what this problem is about, then it's time to add the details (the actual numbers) and start drawing the model.

But don't stop asking questions when you and your students arrive at the solution. As Char Forsten says in her book *Step-by-Step Model Drawing*, "Milk it for all it's worth!" Word problems provide you with the perfect opportunity to practice a lot of different math skills. Once students have solved this problem, for example, ask them:

- *In the end, Cheryl's books are what percent of Brenda's?* $33\frac{1}{3}$ %.

- *What if Brenda had given Cheryl $\frac{1}{2}$ of her books and Cheryl hadn't bought any? What would the ratio of Cheryl's books to Brenda's books have been then?* 7 : 6.

- *After Cheryl makes her purchases, what is the ratio of Cheryl's books to the total number of books?* 1 : 4.

- *How many books would Cheryl have had to buy in order to end up with a 1 : 2 ratio with Brenda?* 30.

You know, I think spending all this time with each problem makes the whole process less mechanical and a lot more interesting. Besides, it keeps kids from just looking at 2 numbers that are given in the word problem, deciding to multiply them because that's the unit you're on this week in school, and assuming they've found the right answer. Using this approach keeps them more accountable.

The ratio of Shakila's CDs to Peggy Foo's CDs was 5 : 3. After Shakila gave Peggy Foo $\frac{1}{2}$ of her CDs, Peggy Foo had 18 more CDs than Shakila started with. How many CDs did Peggy Foo get from Shakila?

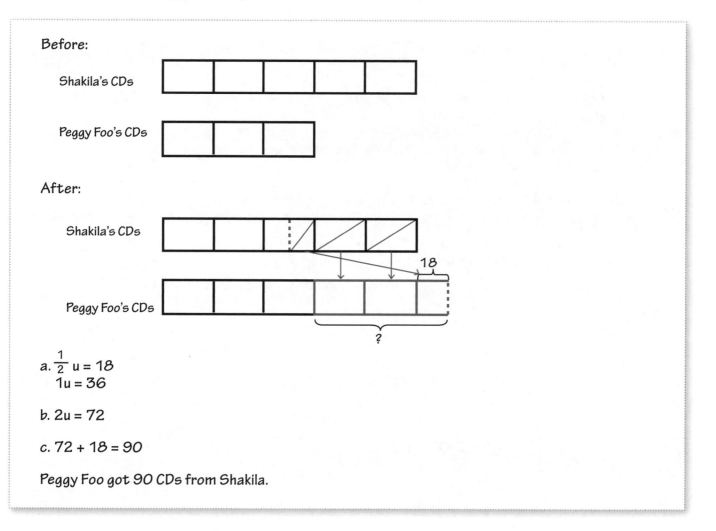

Before:

Shakila's CDs

Peggy Foo's CDs

After:

Shakila's CDs

Peggy Foo's CDs

18

?

a. $\frac{1}{2}$ u = 18
   1u = 36

b. 2u = 72

c. 72 + 18 = 90

Peggy Foo got 90 CDs from Shakila.

I can almost guarantee that some students (and even some adults, for that matter!) will misread this problem. If your original answer was that Peggy Foo got 15 CDs from Shakila, take another look. Did you miss the phrase, "than Shakila started with"?

To emphasize this point with your students, cover up the words "started with" in the problem and ask if leaving those words out affects the answer. Of course, just asking that question will probably give them a giant hint that the answer to your question is, "yes." Make sure you ask them *why* it changes the problem. "Why" should become your new favorite word to use in math class.

Deb baked a total of 144 chocolate chip cookies and peanut butter treats. Initially the ratio of chocolate chip cookies to peanut butter treats was 5 : 3. After Deb's friends ate $\frac{2}{5}$ of her chocolate chip cookies and some of her peanut butter treats, the cookies outnumbered the treats 6 to 1. How many peanut butter treats did she have left?

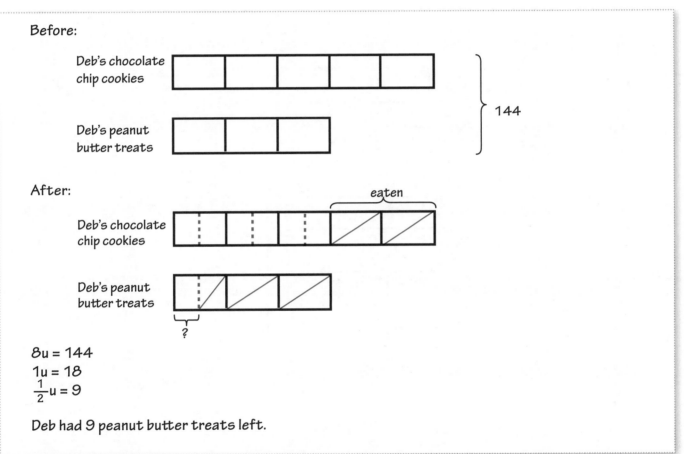

Before:

Deb's chocolate chip cookies

Deb's peanut butter treats

144

After:

eaten

Deb's chocolate chip cookies

Deb's peanut butter treats

?

8u = 144
1u = 18
$\frac{1}{2}$u = 9

Deb had 9 peanut butter treats left.

In this problem you're using ratios to compare quantities. After Deb's friends wolf down all those cookies, you need to make some adjustments to the model to reflect the new ratio of 6 to 1. This is pretty straightforward. Since you have 3 units of chocolate chip cookies left and you want that to reflect the 6 units in the new ratio, just divide each of the units in half.

If you want to increase the level of difficulty of this problem, try changing the 144 cookies in the original problem to 12 dozen.

Elisha, Raynard, and Trece share 92 toy trains. For every train Trece has, Raynard has 3. Elisha has 6 fewer than Raynard. How many trains would Trece need to add to his collection to have $\frac{1}{2}$ as many as Raynard?

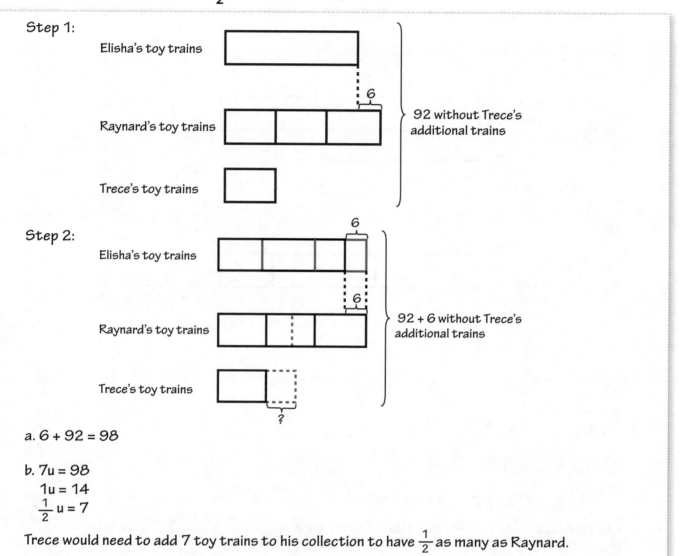

a. $6 + 92 = 98$

b. $7u = 98$
$1u = 14$
$\frac{1}{2}u = 7$

Trece would need to add 7 toy trains to his collection to have $\frac{1}{2}$ as many as Raynard.

Try this problem if you want to see whether your students really comprehend the meaning of ratios. You want them to pick up on the phrase "for every train Trece has, Raynard has 3" and recognize that it's the same as saying that the trains are in a ratio of 1 : 3.

Once I set this one up, I realized I had a total, 92, but I didn't have equal-sized units to divide into that total. In order to come up with those equal units,

I needed to do something to Elisha's unit bar. I could pretend Elisha had the same number of trains as Raynard (which would give me the 3 units that were the same size as the other bars), and then just adjust the total from 92 to 98. From that point, finishing the problem was smooth sailing.

The ratio of Soosen's colored markers to Joyce's was 4 : 1. Joyce had a big art project to work on, so Soosen let her borrow 50 markers. As a result, the ratio of Soosen's markers to Joyce's changed to 2 : 3. If Joyce ended up with 75 markers, how many markers did Soosen start with?

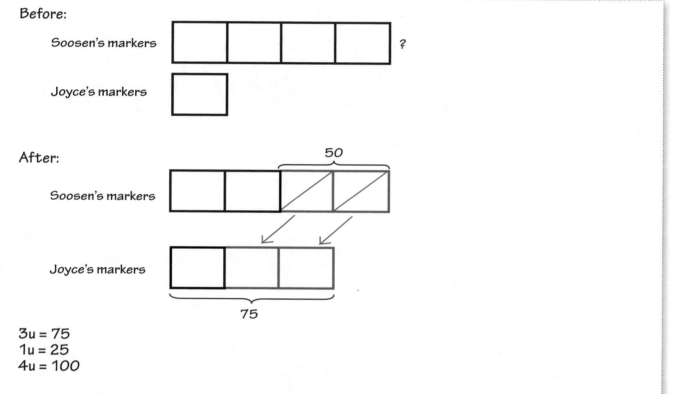

Before:

Soosen's markers

Joyce's markers

After:

50

Soosen's markers

Joyce's markers

75

3u = 75
1u = 25
4u = 100

Soosen started with 100 markers.

Color makes this very clear. The change in the ratios is quite easy to show just by moving some units from Soosen's first model to Joyce's second model.

This problem could also be handled as a mental math problem. Read the problem and tell your kids, "No pencils and no paper. Who can tell me the answer?" When that hand flies up and someone yells out the answer, don't let him stop there. Make that student explain to everyone else what path his brain took to come up with that answer.

Don't rush kids while you're waiting for someone to give you an answer, but if you feel like you're losing them, suggest they focus on Joyce first. (She ended up with 75 markers after Soosen gave her 50 markers. Bet we can figure out how many she started with!)

When Butch and Kent left for their trip, the ratio of Butch's money to Kent's money was 7 : 3. After a short while Butch gave Kent $30, making the new ratio of their cash positions 3 : 2. When they started the trip, how much more money did Butch have than Kent?

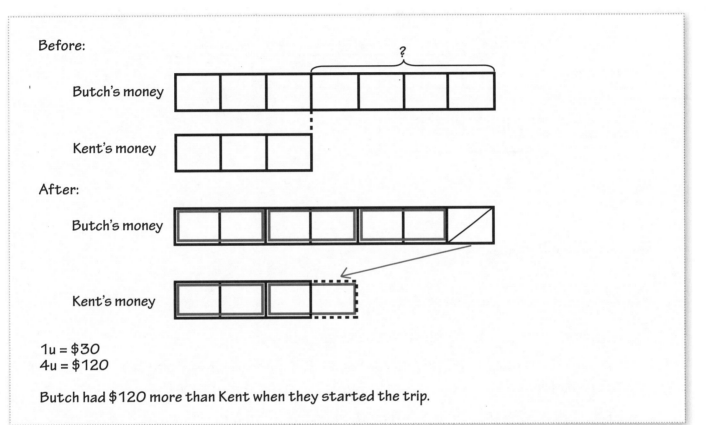

Before:

Butch's money

Kent's money

After:

Butch's money

Kent's money

1u = $30
4u = $120

Butch had $120 more than Kent when they started the trip.

This problem seems similar to the last problem about Soosen and Joyce, but it has a slight twist. In the last problem you just had to move the existing units from one bar model to another to get the desired ratio. That's always what I would consider first when solving this kind of problem. But in this case, when I tried moving one of Butch's units to Kent's second model, Butch then had 6 units and Kent had 4 units. That's when you get one of those "aha" moments. The ratio of 6 to 4 is the same as the ratio of 3 to 2.

The ratio of Mia's balloons to Kiran's was 3 : 5. After Mia was handed 21 more balloons she had twice as many balloons as Kiran. How many balloons did Mia have initially?

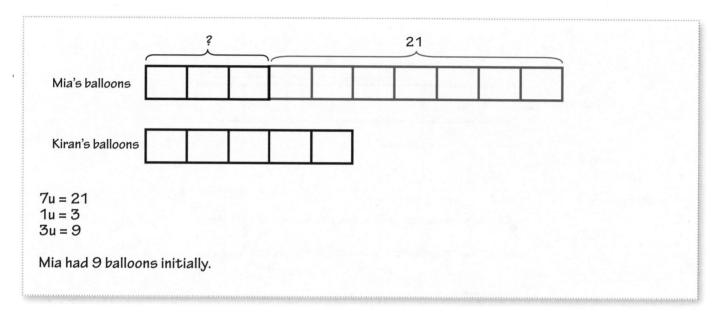

7u = 21
1u = 3
3u = 9

Mia had 9 balloons initially.

As you work through this problem with your students, you might ask:

- *The problem states that after Mia got the additional balloons, she had twice as many balloons as Kiran. How would you express this comparison as a ratio?*

- *The final model shows that Mia has 10 units and Kiran has 5 units. Isn't this supposed to be a ratio of 2 to 1?*

- *How might you show the 2 : 1 more clearly by adding more color to the bar models?*

Now here's a question you should *not* ask. Don't ask, "Is the ratio of 10 to 5 the same as 2 to 1?" It's too easy for them to answer "yes" without even thinking. (They probably won't answer "no" because they've already figured out that the bulk of the time when we ask questions like this, the answer is "yes.")

Another Way

Let's look at how we'd solve this problem if we were using algebra. We have 2 unknowns and one is not specifically described in terms of the other, so we'd probably use a system of linear equations (solving 2 equations that have 2 unknowns).

What equation would show that the ratio of Mia's balloons to Kiran's is 3 : 5? Inevitably I've found that kids will write, "3M = 5K." Wrong. Ask them, "Who has more balloons—Mia or Kiran?" Right: Kiran. So to set the sides up so they're equal, wouldn't we want to multiply the smaller quantity (Mia's balloons) by the larger number/coefficient (5)? So here we go.

M = Mia's initial balloons
K = Kiran's initial balloons

$$\frac{M}{K} = \frac{3}{5}$$

Multiply each side of the equation by 5K and cancel like factors.

$$5\cancel{K} \times \frac{M}{\cancel{K}} = \frac{3}{\cancel{5}} \times \cancel{5}K$$

Our 1st equation:
5M = 3K

Our 2nd equation:
M + 21 = 2K

M = 2K − 21
5(2K − 21) = 3K
10K − 105 = 3K
7K = 105
K = 15

M = 2(15) − 21
M = 9

Wow! Look back at the visual model for this problem and compare it to the algebraic solution. Which one will be easier for your students to really understand? Besides, the algebraic version doesn't give you the opportunities to "milk the problem for all it's worth" and practice previously learned math skills.

I'm not saying you'll never teach how to solve these problems using algebra, because we have to get our kids there. If they have trouble understanding the algebraic solution, though, wouldn't it be great if they had a visual model to fall back on?

Tom and Nancy each collect Civil War books. Initially Tom had 6 times as many books as Nancy. After Tom gave Nancy some of his books for her birthday, the ratio of Tom's books to Nancy's was 9 : 5, and Tom had 12 more books than Nancy. How many Civil War books did Nancy have initially?

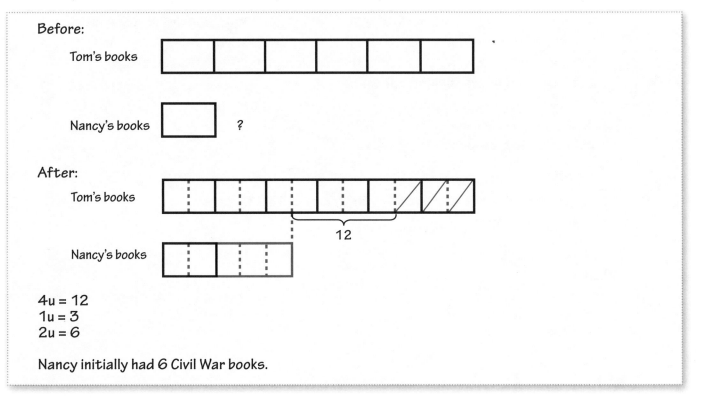

Before:

Tom's books

Nancy's books   ?

After:

Tom's books

12

Nancy's books

4u = 12
1u = 3
2u = 6

Nancy initially had 6 Civil War books.

In many textbook problems, a ratio changes because some number of things goes from one person to another. The easiest version of that type of problem is one in which the unit size doesn't change and you just slide 1 or more of the units from one bar model to another. That's not the case here.

Since the original ratio is 6 : 1 and the new ratio is 9 : 5, I know the size of my units will have to change.

I know that because I know that ratios are based on multiples. If the ratio of Tom's books to Nancy's is 9 : 5, that doesn't necessarily mean Tom has 9 books and Nancy has 5 books. But it does mean that the number of Tom's books is some multiple of 9, and the number of Nancy's books is some multiple of 5. We know that 9 : 5 is just the simplified version of the ratio. So if Tom literally has 18 books, then Nancy must have 10 books. Or maybe Tom has 27 books and Nancy has 15 books.

Okay. Now we're getting somewhere. Let's go back to the original bar model showing the 6 : 1 ratio, and let's subdivide it. I always start by dividing the units in half. Now I have a model that shows 12 : 2. Almost there. Can I take a certain number of units from Tom's model and add them to Nancy's model, so that the resulting ratio ends up being 9 : 5? Bingo! Just moving 3 units from Tom's model to Nancy's model gives me what I need.

You might be thinking, "What if dividing the original units in half hadn't worked?" Sometimes it won't. In that case I try dividing the units in thirds or fourths or whatever gives me the result I need.

Ratio

The ratio of Dave's baseball tickets to Jay's was 1 : 2. Not to be outdone by Jay, Dave decided to buy 6 more tickets, reversing the ratio of Dave's tickets to Jay's and making it 2 : 1. How many tickets did Dave have in the beginning?

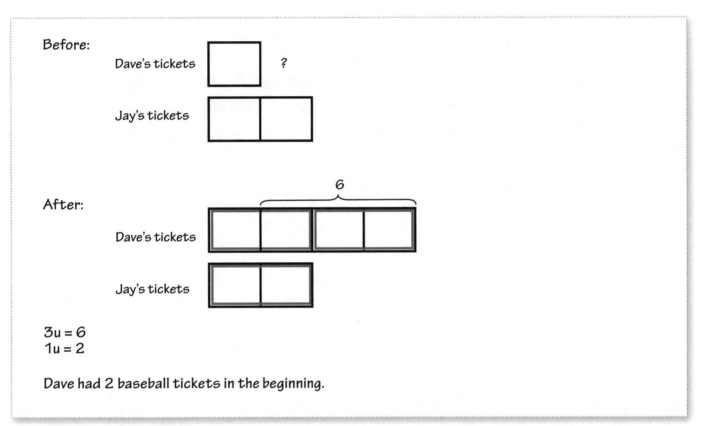

3u = 6
1u = 2

Dave had 2 baseball tickets in the beginning.

When you're solving this problem with your students, ask, "Did Jay's number of tickets change?" No. So let's leave his unit bar unchanged and just adjust Dave's.

In discussing this problem with your class, it's important to point out that the ratio of 4 : 2 is the same as the ratio 2 : 1.

PROBLEM 62

Jill and Jerry shared some plants in a ratio of 5 : 6. Jerry decided to give Jill $\frac{2}{3}$ of his plants, which left him with 21 fewer plants than Jill. How many plants do they have altogether?

PROBLEM 63

The ratio of Bill's money to Bunny's money was 2 : 3. After Bunny spent $\frac{1}{2}$ of her money, Bill had $43 more than Bunny. How much money did Bunny have in the end?

PROBLEM 64

The ratio of Toni's money to Rebecca's money was 5 : 8. Rebecca had $51.30 more than Toni. When Rebecca spent some of her money on a new outfit, she reduced her funds by $\frac{3}{4}$. Does Rebecca have enough money left to buy a white beret that costs $29.95?

PROBLEM 65

Mike had $80 and Dolly had $65. Then they went out to lunch, and each paid $\frac{1}{2}$ of the bill. After they paid for lunch, the ratio of Mike's money to Dolly's money was 7 : 4. How much was their lunch bill?

PROBLEM 66

Althea's and Bing's money totaled $23.76; the ratio of Althea's money to Bing's was 3 to 8. The ratio of Chanise's money to Bing's was 5 to 6. How much more money did Bing have than Chanise?

Satinder can't resist a sale. She recently bought a dress for $93 after it had been discounted 25%. She also purchased shoes that had been marked down 15%; she paid $119 for the shoes. When she got home, how much money did she tell her husband she had saved?

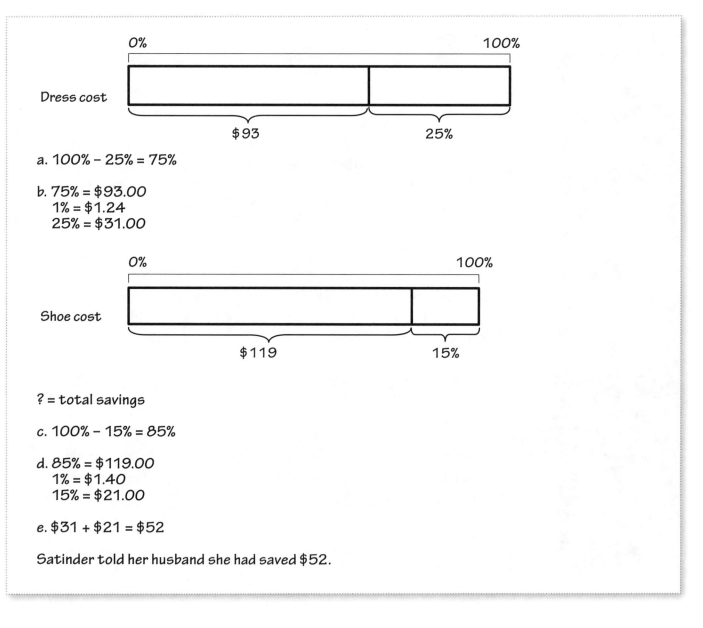

Dress cost

0%   100%

$93   25%

a. 100% – 25% = 75%

b. 75% = $93.00
   1% = $1.24
   25% = $31.00

Shoe cost

0%   100%

$119   15%

? = total savings

c. 100% – 15% = 85%

d. 85% = $119.00
   1% = $1.40
   15% = $21.00

e. $31 + $21 = $52

Satinder told her husband she had saved $52.

When you're solving this it's good to avoid making the 2 bar models the same length. That tends to imply the purchases were equal, and until you do the computation, you don't know if they were or not.

In problems like this one, it's important to point out that if you're receiving, say, a 25% discount on something, then you're paying 75% of the original cost. For this part-whole percent problem, the parts are the sale price and the amount the item was discounted; the whole is the original price of the item.

Always take the time to have what I call "big picture" discussions like this with your students before they jump into the computation. When problem solving becomes less mechanical and more thought provoking, you're building real understanding.

Lydia saved 20% of her income each week. After she received a 10% raise, she was saving an additional $3 each week. What was her original weekly pay?

Before:

0%   100%

Original
weekly pay

20% savings

?

After:

0%   100% 110%

Weekly pay
after raise

20% savings

$3

a. 100% + 10% = 110%

b. To find 20% of 110%:
   100u = 110%
   1u = 1.1%
   20u = 22%

c. The difference in savings (before and after):
   22% – 20% = 2%
   2% = $3.00
   1% = $1.50
   100% = $150.00

Lydia's original weekly pay was $150.

This is a before-and-after problem—a comparison of Lydia's savings before and after her raise. Since the problem gives us that difference as a dollar amount, our task is to figure the difference as a percent.

When starting to solve the problem, ask yourself or your students if one unit bar should be longer than the other. In this case the answer is that the 110% of something should be more than 100% of that same thing. It should also follow that even though the savings is still 20% of the pay, Lydia must be saving more when her pay is greater.

Another Way

If you have a student who knows that 20% of something is the same as $\frac{1}{5}$ of that thing, then that student may take a completely different route to arrive at the answer.

Here's what the student might be thinking:

- If Lydia saves 20% (or $\frac{1}{5}$) of her pay even after the raise, then you could say she saves $\frac{1}{5}$ of her original salary plus $\frac{1}{5}$ of her raise.

- $\frac{1}{5}$ of Lydia's pay after her raise $= \frac{1}{5}$ (her original pay + the raise)

OR

- $\frac{1}{5}$ of Lydia's pay after her raise $= \frac{1}{5}$ of her original pay $+ \frac{1}{5}$ of her raise

   (Sure looks like a fine example of the distributive property to me!)

- If $\frac{1}{5}$ of the raise was $3, then the raise must have been $15.

- If the $15 raise represents 10% (or $\frac{1}{10}$) of Lydia's original pay, then her original pay must have been $150.

Celebrate this child's thinking by saying, "WOW!" (As you know by now, that's short for Whichever One Works.)

69 Percent

Ban Har's stamp collection was 75% the size of Koshu's. After Ban Har sold 40% of his stamps and Koshu sold 20% of her stamps, Ban Har had 140 fewer stamps than Koshu. How many stamps did Ban Har sell?

Before:

Ban Har's stamps — 0% ... 100%

Koshu's stamps — 0% ... 75% ... 100%

Determine what percent of Koshu's original stamps equal Ban Har's remaining stamps.

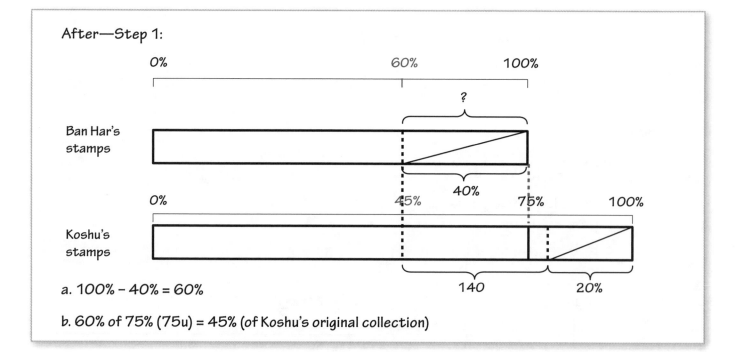

a. 100% − 40% = 60%

b. 60% of 75% (75u) = 45% (of Koshu's original collection)

Express the 140 stamps as a percent of Koshu's original collection and determine the number of stamps in 1% of that collection.

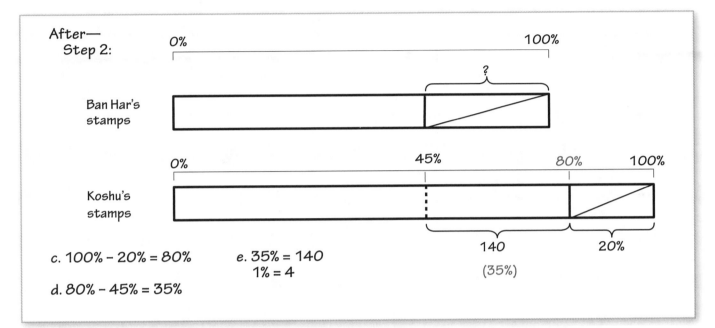

c. 100% – 20% = 80%   e. 35% = 140
                          1% = 4
d. 80% – 45% = 35%

Express Ban Har's sold stamps as a percent of Koshu's original collection and then multiply that percent by 4 (the number of stamps in 1%).

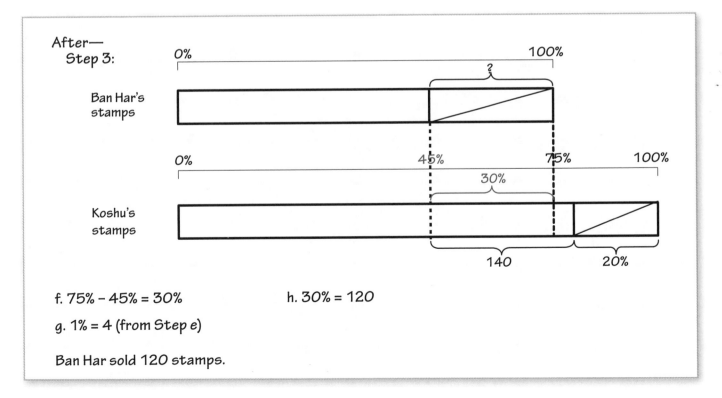

f. 75% – 45% = 30%   h. 30% = 120

g. 1% = 4 (from Step e)

Ban Har sold 120 stamps.

Ban Har's stamp count is described in terms of Koshu's stamp count (Ban Har's collection is 75% of Koshu's), so Koshu's count represents the base or the 100%. Our job is to describe what we know about Ban Har's collection in terms of Koshu's 100% base.

At the Red Sox/Yankees game on Monday night, 65% of the fans were men. Another 25% were women. Of the remainder, 40% were boys and the rest were girls. If 640 boys attended the game, what was the total number of people in attendance?

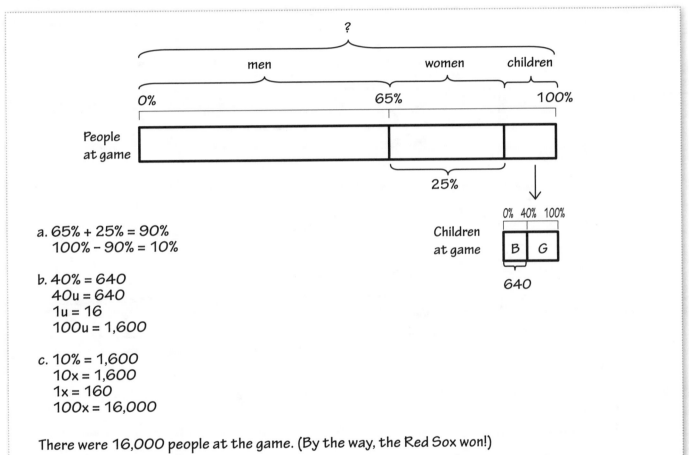

a. 65% + 25% = 90%
   100% – 90% = 10%

b. 40% = 640
   40u = 640
   1u = 16
   100u = 1,600

c. 10% = 1,600
   10x = 1,600
   1x = 160
   100x = 16,000

There were 16,000 people at the game. (By the way, the Red Sox won!)

This is a good example of a part-whole percent problem. The whole is equal to 100% (which we're thinking of as 100 equal units). The "parts" in this problem equal some portion of those 100 units, and together they need to total the 100% (100 units).

Sometimes it helps to think of having a 100% ruler. In this problem there are actually 2 different 100% rulers. The parts of the first one are men, women, and children. Then you break out the children into another model with another 100% ruler; this time you're showing the boys and girls as the parts. From there, you can just work backward, finding the number of children at the game and plugging that number back into the first part of the model.

In a recent school year, 30% of the 120 faculty members were male. The following year several new faculty members were added. The number of females remained unchanged, but the number of males increased to 40% of the faculty. How many new male teachers were added?

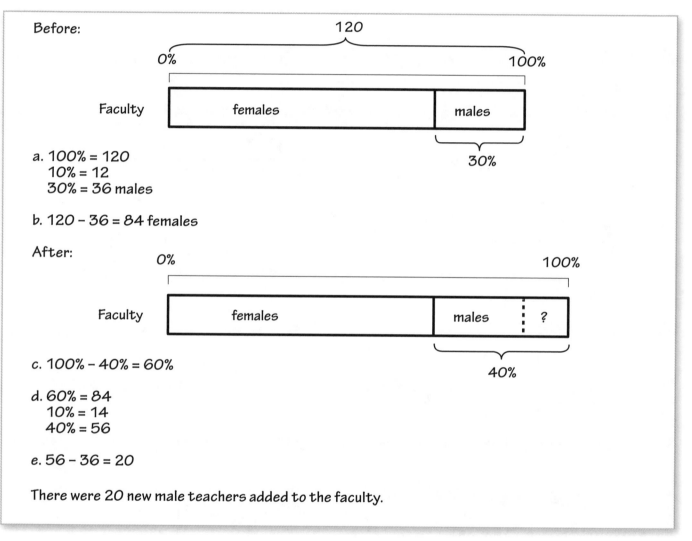

Before:

100

a. 100% = 120
   10% = 12
   30% = 36 males

b. 120 – 36 = 84 females

After:

c. 100% – 40% = 60%

d. 60% = 84
   10% = 14
   40% = 56

e. 56 – 36 = 20

There were 20 new male teachers added to the faculty.

Look at the "Before" model. This is a straightforward part-whole model. You know the whole, and the parts are described as percents of the whole.

When drawing the "After" model, I thought, "Should I make this model longer than the first one?" Sure; I want to be able to visually show that the faculty has grown. I know 40% of the faculty is male. What percent is female? You got it: 60%.

I also know the actual number of female faculty members is the same as before, so I know that 60% of the new faculty is equal to 84. It's worth asking your students to explain why, if the number of female teachers didn't change, the percent of female teachers went from 70% to 60%. If they can explain this (and answer other, similar questions), then they truly understand the concept of percents. Remind them that they've just shown you they're smarter than calculators, which can't do anything more than take the numbers they're given and compute them. Besides, calculators can't explain things!

Percent

Last year, the number of students in Ricky's class was 20% less than the number of students in Donna's class. This year the enrollment in Ricky's class dropped by 25% and the enrollment in Donna's dropped by 10%. Ricky now has 6 fewer students than Donna. How many students did Donna have last year?

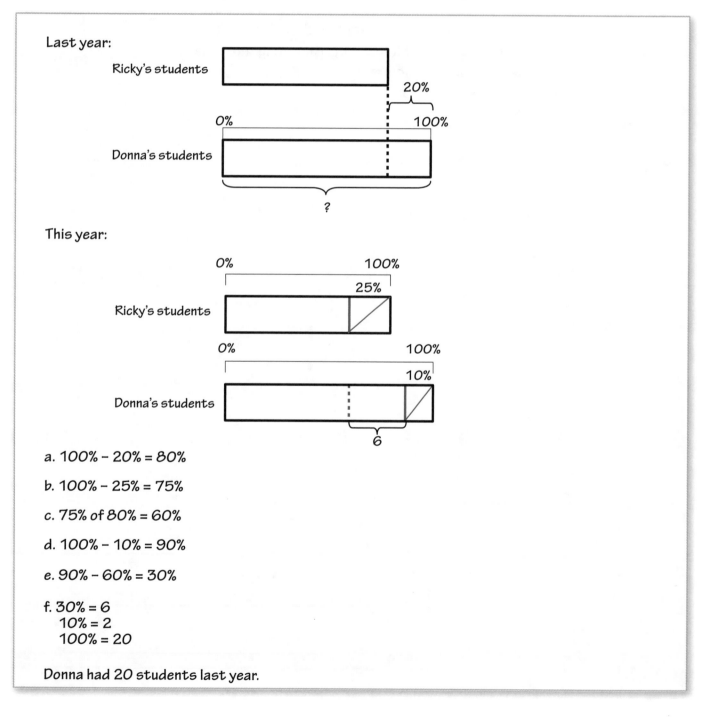

a. 100% − 20% = 80%

b. 100% − 25% = 75%

c. 75% of 80% = 60%

d. 100% − 10% = 90%

e. 90% − 60% = 30%

f. 30% = 6
   10% = 2
   100% = 20

Donna had 20 students last year.

Let's think about this problem. We know that if we say Ricky has 20% fewer students than Donna, that's the same as saying Ricky has 80% of Donna's number of students. Ricky's percent is described in terms of Donna's, so Donna is the 100% base.

Now what we want to do is to describe all the changes that are occurring in Ricky's unit bar as percents of Donna's. This is the key to solving percent problems: *all the unknowns need to be described using the same 100% base.* That's why, when I want to show that the enrollment in Ricky's class dropped 25% in the second year, I'm thinking to myself, "75% of Ricky's 80% is equal to what percent of Donna's bar?"

You can reemphasize this concept—and test your students' thought processes further—with questions like these:

- *If A is 15% less than B, then A is ___% of B? 85%.*

- *If A is 20% less than B, then is B 120% of A?* No! (It's actually 125% of B. Now that's going to get some kids scratching their heads. The key is that the 100% base is switched to A, since B is now described in terms of A.)

If kids are having a hard time with this concept, try walking them through the following:

- A percentage can be thought of as a ratio in which the second number is 100.
  $80\% = 80 : 100$

- A percentage can also be shown as a fraction with 100 in the denominator.
  $80\% = \frac{80}{100}$

- Suppose A = 40 and B = 50.
  A is 80% of B because $\frac{40}{50} = \frac{80}{100}$.

- Now let's compare B to A. $\frac{50}{40} = \frac{5}{4}$ and $\frac{5}{4} = \frac{125}{100}$, so B is 125% of A.

Percent

On December 1, there were 52 more tickets to the Firemen's Ball unsold than sold. At that time the sold tickets represented 30% of the total tickets available. Two weeks later, the percent of sold tickets had increased to 50% of the tickets that were available. How many tickets sold during the 2-week period after December 1?

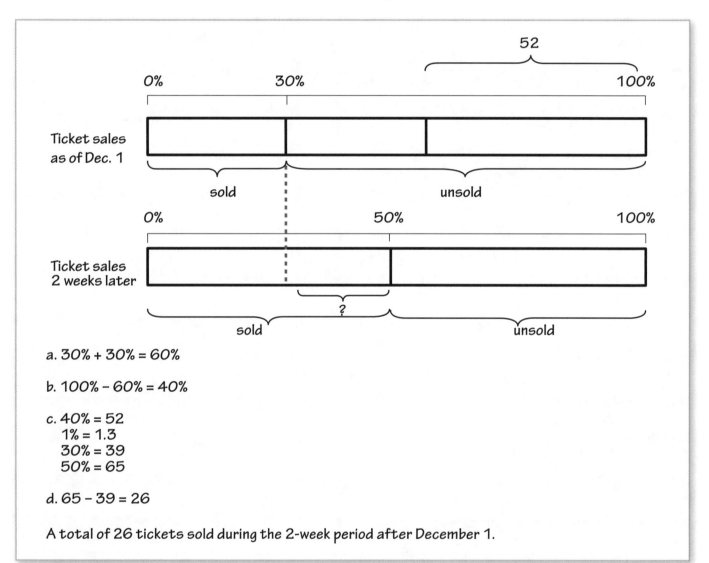

a. 30% + 30% = 60%

b. 100% – 60% = 40%

c. 40% = 52
   1% = 1.3
   30% = 39
   50% = 65

d. 65 – 39 = 26

A total of 26 tickets sold during the 2-week period after December 1.

When you look at the first bar model, it's important to recognize that those first 2 units are the same size (based on the first sentence of the word problem). Once you see that, the problem becomes a simple percent problem. You need to know the value of 1% (1u) in order to find the value of each part of the percent ruler.

After you finish solving this problem together, you might ask your students the following questions:

- *If the tickets continue to sell at the same rate as they did from December 1 through December 15, and if the Firemen's Ball is December 22, will all the tickets have sold before the ball?* No.

- *How many tickets will be left unsold?* 52.

PROBLEM 74

Initially, of all the members of the school band, 30% were boys. After some of the boys dropped out, only 20% of the remaining band members were boys. If the band had 80 members in the beginning, how many boys left the band?

PROBLEM 75

Initially, there were 4,800 plants for sale at Walker Farm. Of those, 30% were annuals and the rest were perennials. By noon on Saturday, $\frac{2}{5}$ of the annuals had sold and 768 of the perennials had sold. What percent of the remaining plants were annuals?

PROBLEM 76

Carrie mailed 20% more holiday cards this year than she mailed last year. If she mailed 13 more cards this year than last year, how many did she mail last year?

PROBLEM 77

At first Priscilla had 5 times as many jellybeans as Camilla. Then the girls decided to share some with their friend Scarlett. After Priscilla gave Scarlett 12% of her jellybeans and Camilla gave Scarlett 25% of hers, Scarlett had a total of 102 jellybeans. That was 50% more than what she started with. How many jellybeans did Camilla give Scarlett?

Sandy was buying new notebooks and pens for her home office. At one store she bought 2 notebooks and 2 pens for $13.14. At another store she found the exact same products and pricing; this time she paid $25.08 for 5 notebooks and 2 pens. How much did each notebook cost?

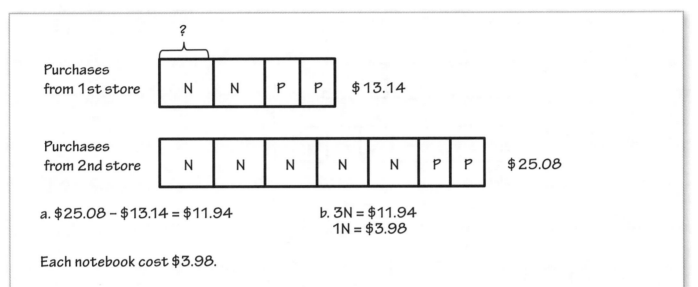

a. $25.08 – $13.14 = $11.94

b. 3N = $11.94
   1N = $3.98

Each notebook cost $3.98.

You can use model drawing to solve problems with 2 unknowns, like this one. The idea is to create a visual model of the equations you would use if you were solving the problem using a system of linear equations.

Start by creating discrete models with units in 2 different sizes. Use one label to identify each of the smaller units and a different label to identify each of the larger ones. Place the total for each unit bar to the right of that bar.

What you want to do is to "subtract" one model (or equation) from the other one with the goal of eliminating one of the unknowns. In this case, I can see from the model for the first store that the total of the 2 "N" units and the 2 "P" units in the model for the second store is $13.14. So I know the remaining 3 "N" units must equal the difference between $25.08 and $13.14.

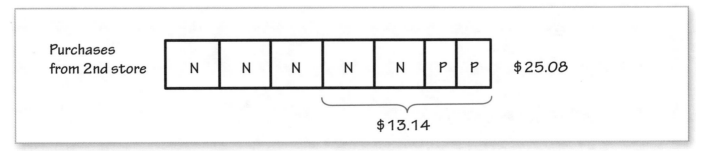

There are 73 children at the playground. One-third of the boys and $\frac{2}{7}$ of the girls are swimming in the pool. If there are 22 kids in the pool in all, how many boys are there at the playground?

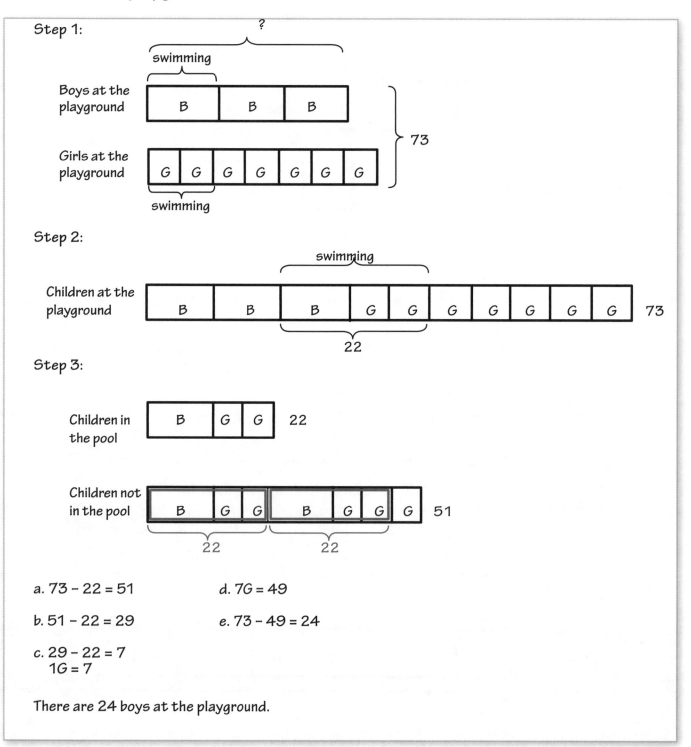

Step 1:

Step 2:

Step 3:

a. 73 − 22 = 51

b. 51 − 22 = 29

c. 29 − 22 = 7
   1G = 7

d. 7G = 49

e. 73 − 49 = 24

There are 24 boys at the playground.

This problem is similar to the infamous "goggle" problem that Dr. Yeap Bar Har had on his blog, www.singaporemathz4kidz.blogspot.com. I started out by approaching it as a comparison problem, as you can see in Step 1. The problem here was that the unknowns are not described in terms of each other, so it's not a comparison problem. Besides, I had no idea how to show there were 22 kids in the pool. Then I started to hear Ban Har in my head: "Be persistent. What else do you know?"

That took me to Step 2, in which I used a part-whole model. Now I could show the 22 kids in the pool. Finally, a light went off in my head. I realized I had 2 unknowns, so I needed another bar model. I had the answer to the question, "What else do you know?" I knew something about the kids *not* in the pool! That brought me to Step 3.

Now it was a matter of "subtracting" the "Children in the pool" model from the "Children not in the pool" model—and doing that twice to get to just 1 variable.

Once I got that far, I plugged the numbers back into the model and completed the calculation to answer the question.

Another Way

I'm sure you've already realized that instead of doing this repeated subtraction I could have just doubled the "Children in the pool" model to make it look like the following. Then I would have subtracted only once.

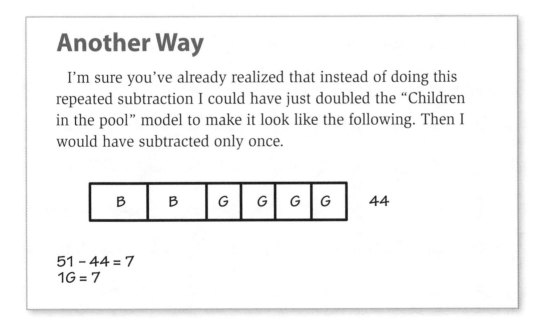

51 – 44 = 7
1G = 7

On Tuesday, Jenn picks up 8 bagels and 3 cups of coffee at the Bagel Mill and spends $14.45. On Wednesday, it's Jamila's turn; she spends $16.15 for 4 bagels and 5 cups of coffee. What does the Bagel Mill charge for a cup of coffee?

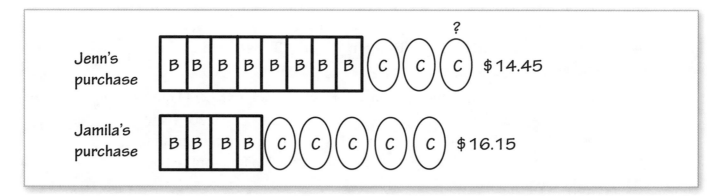

When you are trying to show 2 distinct unknowns in your model, don't be afraid to use a different shape for each unknown as I've done here.

This problem isn't as easy as the last one because even after I "subtract" one model from the other, I still have 2 unknowns. Even repeated subtraction doesn't work. You need to be able to "clear the deck" of one of the unknowns. Here's a hint on how to get there: think "common multiple."

Suppose I want to eliminate the bagels. Jenn purchased 8 and Jamila purchased 4, so the common multiple is 8. Let's make both models have 8 bagels in them. Just imagine that Jamila doubles her order. (Remember to double the total.)

From Jenn's purchase, we know that 8 bagels and 3 coffees equal $14.45, so now we can eliminate those bagels and coffees from the left side of the doubled order and subtract the $14.45 from the total cost of the order. That leaves us with units that are all coffees—all the same unknown—so we can easily find the answer.

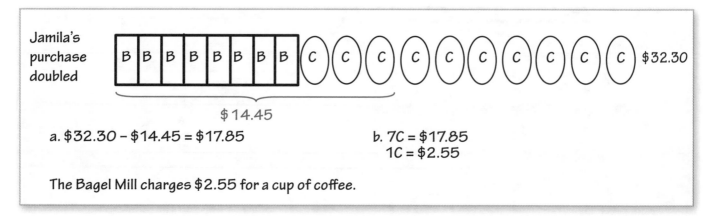

a. $32.30 − $14.45 = $17.85

b. 7C = $17.85
   1C = $2.55

The Bagel Mill charges $2.55 for a cup of coffee.

Two Unknowns

Two groups of parents and kids went to the Saturday matinee. Caitlin bought 2 adult tickets and 5 kid tickets. She paid a total of $35.50. Torri bought 3 adult tickets and 2 kid tickets for the same show and paid $28.50. What would be the cost of 2 adult tickets plus 3 kid tickets?

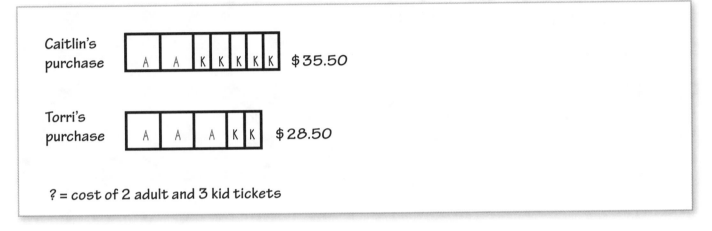

Caitlin's purchase   A A K K K K K $35.50

Torri's purchase   A A A K K $28.50

? = cost of 2 adult and 3 kid tickets

Hmm. It's not so easy this time. To help, I've used color to distinguish the unknowns in the model. If my goal is to get the same number of "A" units in both models, once again I need to think in terms of common multiples. Let's triple Caitlin's purchase and double Torri's purchase.

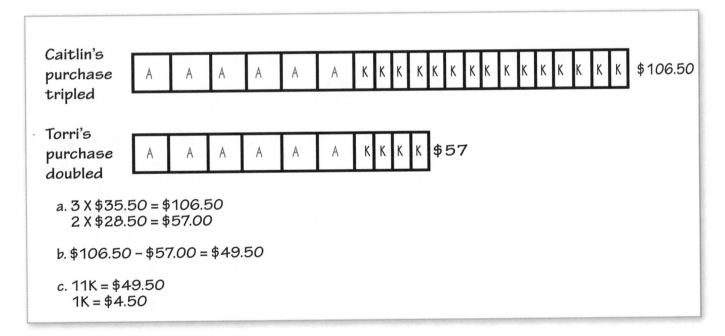

Caitlin's purchase tripled   A A A A A A K K K K K K K K K K K K K K K $106.50

Torri's purchase doubled   A A A A A A K K K K $57

a. 3 X $35.50 = $106.50
   2 X $28.50 = $57.00

b. $106.50 – $57.00 = $49.50

c. 11K = $49.50
   1K = $4.50

Now let's look back at the first model.

d. 5K = $22.50

e. 2A + $22.50 = $35.50
   2A = $13.00

f. 3K = $13.50

g. $13.00 + $13.50 = $26.50

The cost of 2 adult tickets plus 3 kid tickets would be $26.50.

Two Unknowns

At Grappelli's Pizza, Lalanya bought 2 cheese pizzas, 1 pepperoni-mushroom pizza, and 1 pizza with "the works" for a total of $34.90. Lou purchased 3 with "the works" and 1 pepperoni-mushroom pizza for a total of $46. Noele told them she knew the pizza with "the works" cost $1.40 less than 2 cheese pizzas, but she didn't know the cost of the pepperoni-mushroom pizza. Can you help her find the cost of the pepperoni-mushroom pizza?

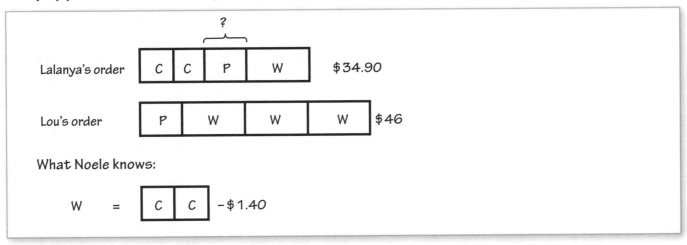

These models are relatively easy to write. You'll notice that the third piece is starting to look more like an equation than a typical unit bar. I think you'll see there's a nice opportunity to do some substituting here. You could either replace the "W" in the first model with "CC – $1.40" or replace the "CC" in the first model with "W + $1.40." I chose the second option and got:

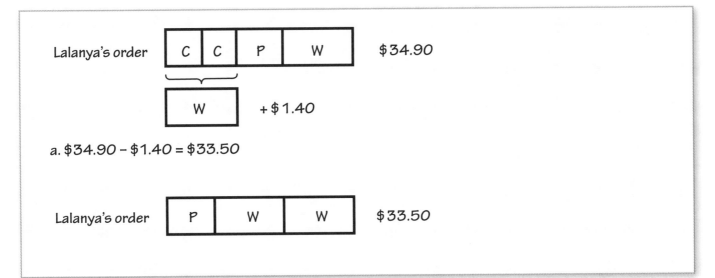

Therefore, in the second model I have:

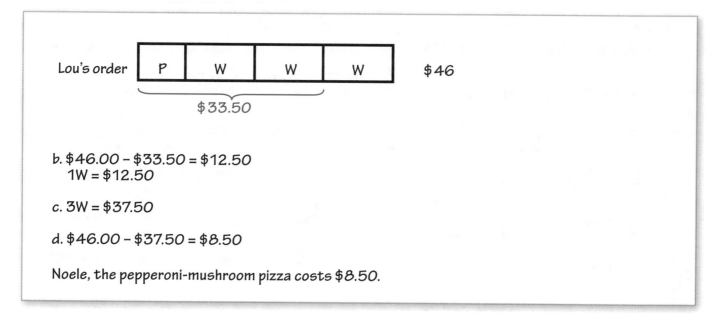

b. $46.00 – $33.50 = $12.50
   1W = $12.50

c. 3W = $37.50

d. $46.00 – $37.50 = $8.50

Noele, the pepperoni-mushroom pizza costs $8.50.

If you want to challenge some students, ask them to figure the cost of a slice of each type of pizza. Tell them to assume that Grappelli's divides each pizza into 6 slices and then rounds up the price of each slice to the nearest half dollar.

PROBLEM

83

At the Corner Market, 3 oranges and 1 apple cost $1.86, and 2 oranges and 3 apples cost $2.15. Find the cost of 1 apple.

PROBLEM

84

The sum of 2 whole numbers is 28. When one of the numbers is tripled and added to the other number, the sum is then 50. What are the 2 numbers?

PROBLEM

85

Soren and Cassie each donated the same amount of money to NPR. Before they made their donations, Soren had $178 and Cassie had $670. After donating, Cassie had 5 times as much money as Soren. How much money did they each donate?

PROBLEM

86

Kate and Melissa both went to the same store to buy eggs and bread for their families. Kate bought 3 dozen eggs and 5 loaves of bread; she spent $30.07. Melissa purchased 2 dozen eggs and 2 loaves of bread; she spent $14.74. What is the store charging for a dozen eggs?

87 Algebra

If $\frac{3}{5}$ of a number is x, then what is $\frac{2}{3}$ of the number? Express your answer in terms of x.

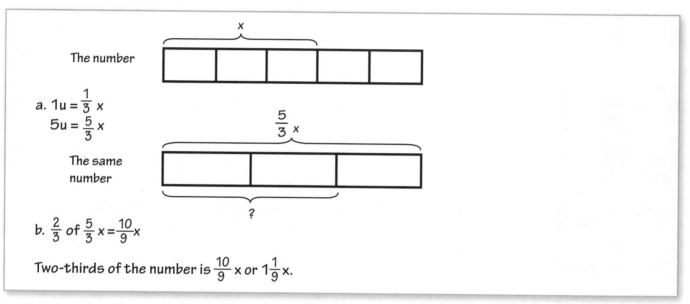

a. $1u = \frac{1}{3}x$

$5u = \frac{5}{3}x$

b. $\frac{2}{3}$ of $\frac{5}{3}x = \frac{10}{9}x$

Two-thirds of the number is $\frac{10}{9}x$ or $1\frac{1}{9}x$.

If students need more help with Step b, try showing them this area model. Here each square represents 1 whole; the 5 tall rectangular bars (without the shading) represent $\frac{5}{3}$ or $1\frac{2}{3}$.

If I want $\frac{2}{3}$ of those $\frac{5}{3}$ strips, I just divide the squares horizontally. The big squares are now divided into ninths (9 units of equal size); $\frac{2}{3}$ of them are $\frac{10}{9}$ (the area shaded red).

Ming has a rectangular piece of fabric that is 26*y* inches by 15*y* inches. She wants to use the fabric to cover a stool. She cuts 6-inch squares from each corner of the fabric so she can bring those open corners together. (The result will look like the lid of a box.) She decides she also wants to add trim to the outside edge once the side flaps are sewn together in the corners. How many inches of trim does she need? Express your answer in terms of *y*.

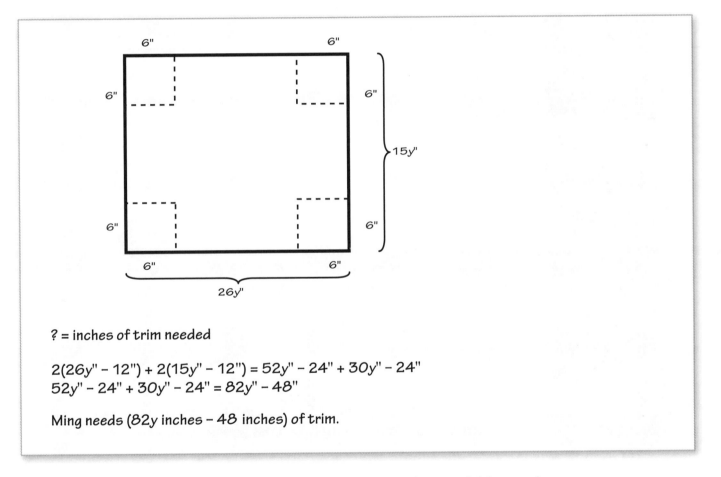

? = inches of trim needed

2(26y" – 12") + 2(15y" – 12") = 52y" – 24" + 30y" – 24"
52y" – 24" + 30y" – 24" = 82y" – 48"

Ming needs (82y inches – 48 inches) of trim.

   I've included this problem just as a reminder that a bar model is not always the best visual to use for a problem. For area and perimeter problems, for example, a more realistic, 2-dimensional model is often better.

PROBLEM 89

Inese had collected 120 recipes. Once she got *r* more from a friend, she then had twice as many as Sharon. How many recipes does Sharon have? Express your answer in terms of *r*.

PROBLEM 90

Gerry divided his Porsche model cars equally into 4 sets. If each set ended up with *k* cars, how many cars did he have? Express your answer in terms of *k*.

PROBLEM 91

If $\frac{2}{3}$ of a number is *m*, what is the number? Express your answer in terms of *m*.

PROBLEM 92

Char took her friends out for ice cream. Her friends ordered 5 cones for $3.25 each and one sundae for $*y*. If Char gave the waitress $40, how much change did she get back? Express your answer in terms of *y*.

PROBLEM 93

Terri won $250 playing bingo. She gave $*b* to each of her 3 friends. How much money did she have left? Express your answer in terms of *b*.

PROBLEM 94

John had 28 books. His friend Kath had *x* times as many books as John. How many books did they have altogether? Express your answer in terms of *x*.

PROBLEM 95

If Patt had *y* cookies and Flo had 2 cookies, Patt had how many times as many cookies as Flo? Express your answer in terms of *y*.

PROBLEM 96

Miguel bought 6 pounds of coffee. He gave the clerk $*h* and received $4.26 in change. How much per pound did the coffee cost? Express your answer in terms of *h*.

PROBLEM 97

Betty has $5*c*. Jim has twice as much as Betty, and Laureen has $4 more than Jim. How much do they have altogether? Express your answer in terms of *c*.

Putting It All Together

Working Backward & Forward from the Model

In working with students, I've found that usually there are only 2 stages that they find challenging when they solve word problems with model drawing:

1. Translating the words and numbers into a bar model. *This stage is tricky for some but doable for most once they've had some practice.*

2. Adjusting the model(s) if necessary and/or deciding what computation to complete first. *If someone is having difficulties, it's usually with this stage. Remember: "Listen and the model will talk to you."*

Rarely have I found anyone having problems with the computation stage.

So let's agree that some people are going to need more practice with adjusting the model and deciding where to begin the computation. For those students, consider creating the bar model and letting the students work the model backward and forward.

To work it backward, ask your students to fire up their creative juices and write a word problem that matches the model. If you use this in your class, it could become a creative-writing activity. It would be fun to see the variety of stories your kids could come up with. I've actually seen one of these models turned into a page-long "story problem."

To work it forward, encourage your students to practice "listening to the model." Tell them to look for a place in the model where some number appears as the total of some equal units. Or maybe the students are doing a comparison problem in which the units in one of the models are not the same size as the units in the other models; by now you know they need to subdivide the units to get units of the same size in each model. Then, when they complete the computation, they'll come up with the value represented by the question mark. (Let's hope that when they reach this point, your students' results aren't all different!)

The following models include the computations that would lead to a solution for each one. You and your students are on your own for the creative-writing part of these problems.

This type of activity gives you a great opportunity to practice model drawing in a totally different way. Have fun with it!

1

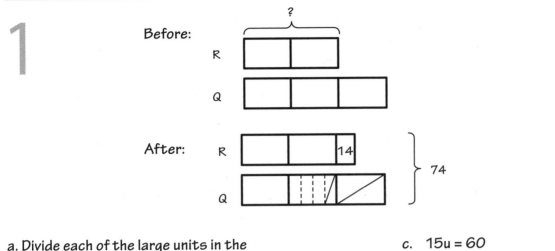

Before:

R

Q

After:

R [| |14]

Q

} 74

a. Divide each of the large units in the "After" model into fourths.

b. 74 – 14 = 60

c.   15u = 60
    1u = 4
    8u = 32

2

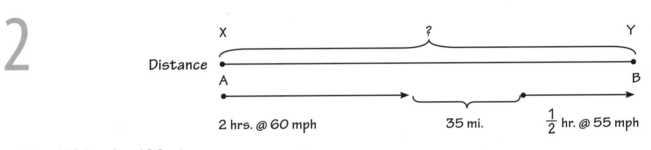

Distance

X ————————?———————— Y

A ————————————→ B

2 hrs. @ 60 mph   35 mi. $\frac{1}{2}$ hr. @ 55 mph

a. 2 hrs. X 60 mph = 120 mi.

b. $\frac{1}{2}$ hr. X 55 mph = 27.5 mi.

c. 120 mi. + 35 mi. + 27.5 mi. = 182.5 mi.

3

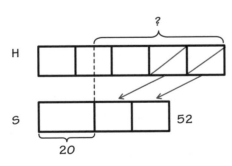

H

S [| | |52]

20

a. 52 – 20 = 32

b. 2u = 32
    1u = 16
    5u = 80

c. 80 – 20 = 60

4

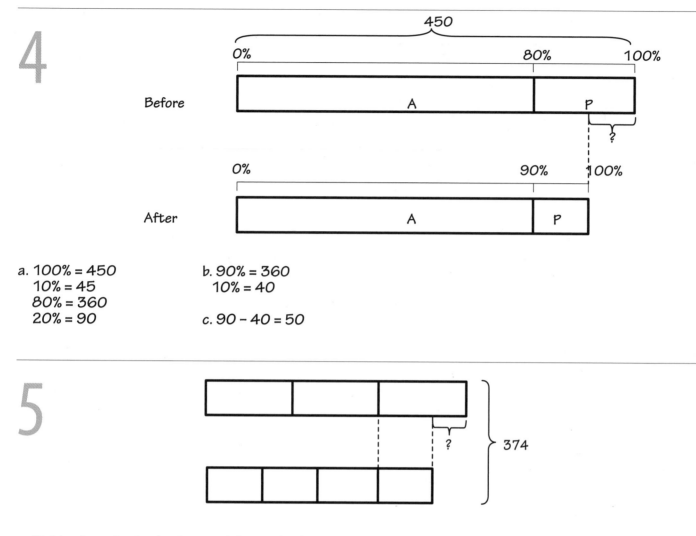

Before

After

a. 100% = 450
   10% = 45
   80% = 360
   20% = 90

b. 90% = 360
   10% = 40

c. 90 – 40 = 50

5

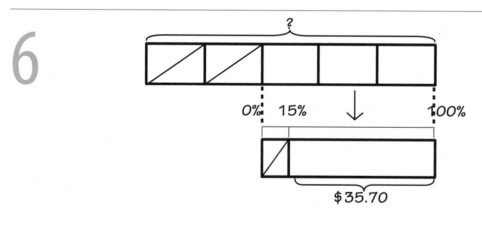

a. Divide the units in the 1st model into thirds.

b. Divide the units in the 2nd model into halves.

c. 17u = 374
   1u = 22

6

a. 100% – 15% = 85%

b. 85% = $35.70
   1% = $0.42
   100% = $42.00

c. $42.00 ÷ 3 = $14.00

d. 5 X $14.00 = $70.00

Final Exam

In this book, we've used model drawing to solve some pretty complex problems. I hope you've taken the time to try these problems on your own before reading any clues I added—and that sometimes you came up with completely different ways to reach the same solutions. I also hope that working through these examples has challenged you to think about word problems in a new way. You know that taking things step by step will help you solve a lot of problems that look overwhelming at first. You know that you need to always think about what you know—which sometimes is more than what the problem directly says. And you know that you need to "listen to the model" and let it speak to you.

Now, are you ready for the final exam? Here's a chance to see just how much you really know. (If you get stuck, don't worry. Solutions begin on page 143.)

The Majestic Theater has a seating capacity of 420. At a Saturday matinee $\frac{1}{4}$ of the seats were sold to adults, $\frac{2}{5}$ to senior citizens, and the rest to children. If the management sold all the seats that day, how many children's tickets did they sell?

Find 3 consecutive odd integers such that twice the first number is equal to 17 more than the third number.

The sum of Cathy's and Tony's ages is 65. Eight years ago Cathy's age was $\frac{2}{5}$ of Tony's age. How old are they now?

Tim loved hot dogs and bought 5 of them at the hot dog stand. If he gave the owner $h and got $12.05 in change, what was the cost of a single hot dog? Express your answer in terms of h.

Travis has $\frac{1}{5}$ as many books as Manda and $\frac{2}{3}$ as many books as Dan. If Dan has 7 more books than Travis, how many books does Manda have?

Beck had $5 less than Delmar. After Beck went shopping for new clothes and spent $\frac{2}{3}$ of her money, she then had $35 less than Delmar. How much money did Beck have left?

Originally, Barbie and Maggie had the same number of plants in their homes. After Barbie gave away 17 plants and 5 of Maggie's died, the ratio of Barbie's plants to Maggie's plants was 4 : 7. How many plants did they each start with?

The sales team at Latti Motors sold 2 used cars on Monday. One car sold for $3,800, which resulted in a profit of 25% over the buying price. The other car sold for $2,480, which represented a 20% loss. Find the total loss or profit from these 2 sales.

Meg, Zach, and Josh all had summer jobs. During the first week of the summer, the ratio of Meg's earnings to Zach's earnings was 5 : 12. The comparison of Zach's and Josh's earnings was 3 : 2. If Meg ended up with $21 less than Zach that week, how much did Josh earn during the same week?

During the Pie Challenge at the County Fair, a total of 50 apple and blueberry pies were entered into the contest. Initially the ratio of apple pies to blueberry pies was 4 : 1. Later the judges disqualified some of the blueberry pies, leaving 5 times as many apple pies as blueberry pies to be judged. How many blueberry pies were disqualified?

Appendix

12

Four people at work were born on consecutive days in July. The sum of the 4 dates is 86. On what dates do their birthdays fall?

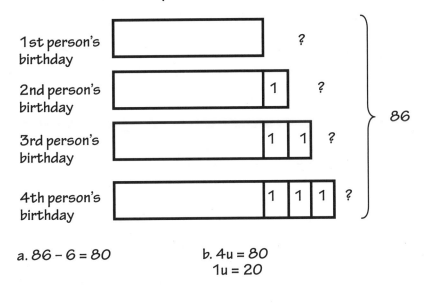

a. 86 − 6 = 80

b. 4u = 80
   1u = 20

The birthdays are July 20, 21, 22, and 23.

13

Jan shopped at 4 different stores. When she looked at her receipts, she realized that the amounts she had spent in the 4 stores were consecutive multiples of 7. The total amount she spent was $98 more than twice what she spent at the second store. How much did Jan spend at the second store?

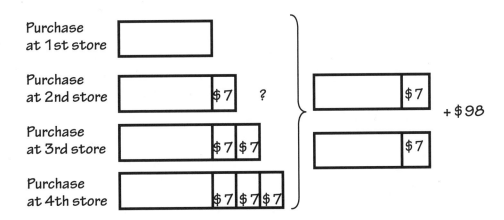

Cross off equivalent units from each side of the model. Then compute.

a. 4 X $7 = $28

b. $98 − $28 = $70

c. 2u = $70
   1u = $35

d. $35 + $7 = $42

Jan spent $42 at the second store.

14

The lengths of the sides of a quadrilateral are consecutive multiples of 6. If the perimeter of the quadrilateral is 156 inches, how long is the shortest side?

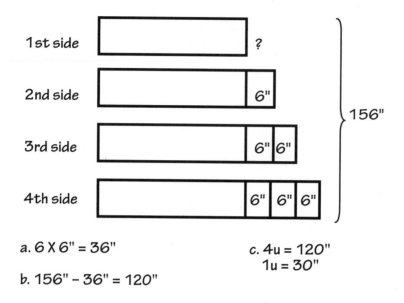

a. 6 X 6" = 36"

c. 4u = 120"
1u = 30"

b. 156" – 36" = 120"

The shortest side is 30 inches.

31

Lorie spent $\frac{3}{5}$ of her money on gifts for Luann and Joan. Luann's gift cost 3 times as much as Joan's gift. If Lorie had $12 left after she made her purchases, how much did Luann's gift cost?

Step 1:

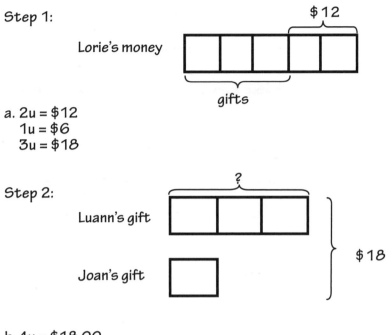

a. 2u = $12
   1u = $6
   3u = $18

Step 2:

b. 4x = $18.00
   1x = $4.50
   3x = $13.50

Luann's gift cost $13.50.

32

The sum of 2 numbers is 10. The difference between the 2 numbers is $\frac{1}{3}$ of the greater number. What are the numbers?

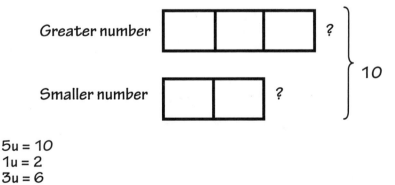

5u = 10
1u = 2
3u = 6
2u = 4

The 2 numbers are 6 and 4.

33

Ted and Barbara had the same amount of money. Ted gave $\frac{1}{3}$ of his to Tillie and Barbara gave $\frac{1}{4}$ of hers to Maddy. In the end Ted had $8 less than Barbara. How much did Ted and Barbara each have originally?

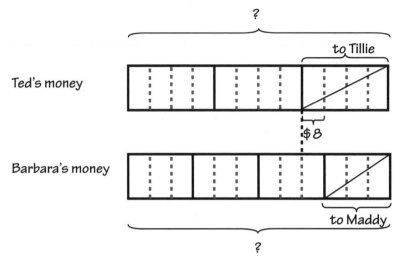

1u = $8
12u = $96

Ted and Barbara each had $96 originally.

34

Michele had 3 times as many cookies as Sally. Michele got really hungry in the afternoon and ate 20 of her cookies. Afterward Michele had only half as many cookies as Sally. How many cookies did Sally have?

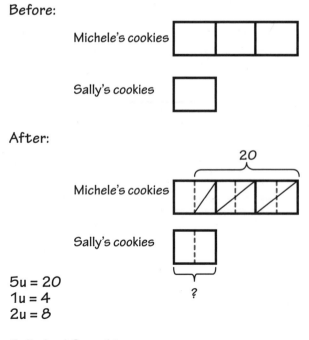

5u = 20
1u = 4
2u = 8

Sally had 8 cookies.

35

Ebby had a job mowing lawns. After 3 days she still had $\frac{5}{7}$ of the lawns left to mow. In the next 3 days she increased her speed and mowed $1\frac{1}{2}$ times as many as in the first 3 days, but she still had 6 more lawns to mow. How many lawns did she have to mow in total?

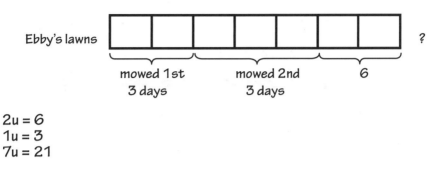

2u = 6
1u = 3
7u = 21

Ebby had 21 lawns to mow in total.

41

At the beginning of the week, the difference between Ricardo's money and Liliana's money was $12.50. By the end of the week they had each spent half of their money, and they had a total of $137.85 left. How much did each of them start with? Who had the most money?

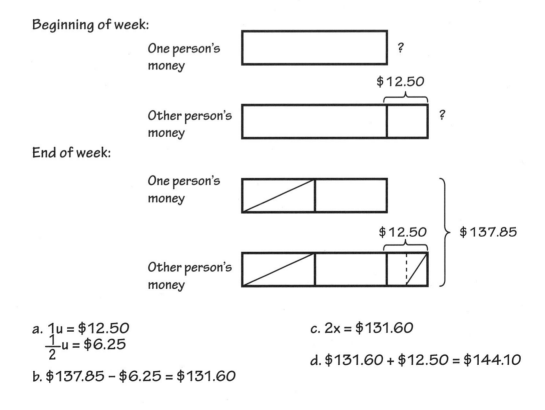

a. 1u = $12.50
$\frac{1}{2}$u = $6.25

b. $137.85 – $6.25 = $131.60

c. 2x = $131.60

d. $131.60 + $12.50 = $144.10

One person started the week with $131.60, and the other started with $144.10. There is no way to know who had which amount, so you can't answer the question about who had the most money.

Model Drawing for Challenging Word Problems

42

Matt has 0.75 times as much money as Todd and Todd has 0.8 times as much as Katie. If Katie has $128.80, how much do they have altogether?

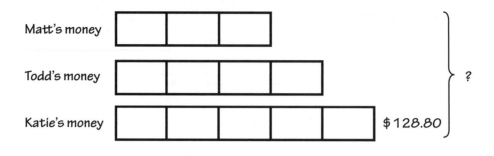

a. $0.75 = \dfrac{3}{4}$

   $0.8 = \dfrac{4}{5}$

b. $5u = \$128.80$

   $1u = \$25.76$

   $12u = \$309.12$

Together they have $309.12.

43

Samantha was making bags for a crafts fair. She bought 12 yards of fabric at $9.79 per yard for the outside of the bags, and she bought 9 yards of fabric at $6.95 per yard to use for the bag linings. She sold all the finished bags for a total of $318.78. What was her profit?

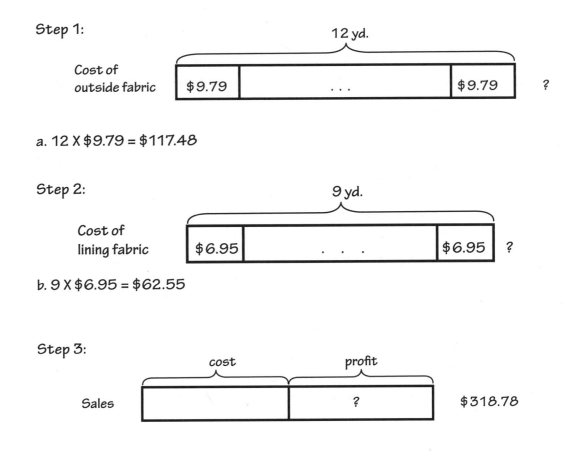

Step 1:

a. 12 X $9.79 = $117.48

Step 2:

b. 9 X $6.95 = $62.55

Step 3:

c. $117.48 + $62.55 = $180.03

d. $318.78 – $180.03 = $138.75

Samantha's profit was $138.75.

44

Shernece decided everyone on her holiday shopping list would get a hat or a scarf. The hats cost $18.95 each, and the scarves cost $28.95 each; she purchased 5 more hats than scarves. If her total purchases came to $477.95, how many hats did she buy?

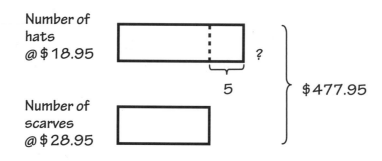

a. 5 × $18.95 = $94.75   b. $477.95 – $94.75 = $383.20

If the number of hats that are left equals the number of scarves, then the average cost of these items would be ($18.95 + $28.95) ÷ 2, or $23.95.

c. $383.20 ÷ $23.95 = 16   e. 8 + 5 = 13

d. 2u = 16
   1u = 8

Shernece bought 13 hats.

50

Mark and Liz entered a scooter race of 72 miles. Mark arrived late and started the race 30 minutes later than Liz, but he whizzed down the road at 18 miles per hour. If they finished the race at the same time, what was Liz's average speed?

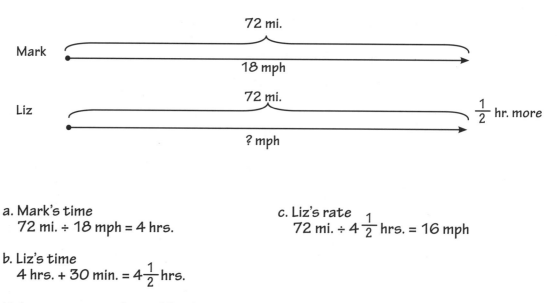

a. Mark's time
   72 mi. ÷ 18 mph = 4 hrs.

c. Liz's rate
   72 mi. ÷ $4\frac{1}{2}$ hrs. = 16 mph

b. Liz's time
   4 hrs. + 30 min. = $4\frac{1}{2}$ hrs.

Liz's average speed was 16 miles per hour.

51

Fernando and Ron each drove from Peterborough to Honesdale. They started at the same time, and each traveled at a uniform speed. When Fernando reached Honesdale, Ron was still 78 miles away. Ron reached Honesdale $1\frac{1}{2}$ hours after Fernando got there. If the 2 towns are 390 miles apart, at what speed was Fernando traveling?

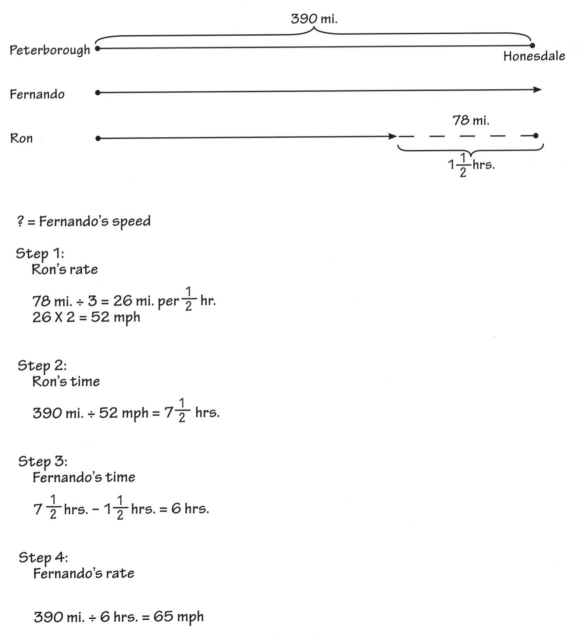

? = Fernando's speed

Step 1:
   Ron's rate

   78 mi. ÷ 3 = 26 mi. per $\frac{1}{2}$ hr.
   26 X 2 = 52 mph

Step 2:
   Ron's time

   390 mi. ÷ 52 mph = $7\frac{1}{2}$ hrs.

Step 3:
   Fernando's time

   $7\frac{1}{2}$ hrs. – $1\frac{1}{2}$ hrs. = 6 hrs.

Step 4:
   Fernando's rate

   390 mi. ÷ 6 hrs. = 65 mph

Fernando was traveling at 65 miles per hour.

52

Finn and Ella started traveling at the same time, from the same spot, but in opposite directions. After 2 hours they were 176 miles apart. If Finn's average speed was 2 miles per hour faster than Ella's, what was Ella's average speed?

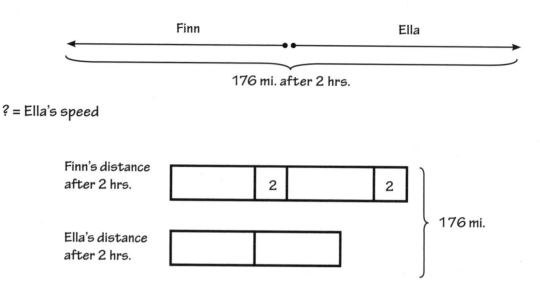

? = Ella's speed

a. 2 hrs. X 2 mph = 4 mi.

b. 176 mi. – 4 mi. = 172 mi.

c. 4u = 172 mi.
   1u = 43 mph

Ella's average speed was 43 miles per hour.

62

Jill and Jerry shared some plants in a ratio of 5 : 6. Jerry decided to give Jill $\frac{2}{3}$ of his plants, which left him with 21 fewer plants than Jill. How many plants do they have altogether?

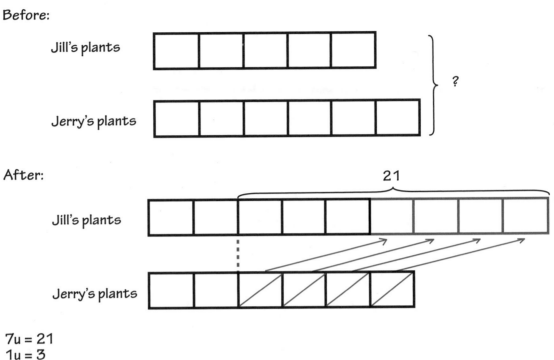

Before:

Jill's plants

Jerry's plants

?

After:

21

Jill's plants

Jerry's plants

7u = 21
1u = 3
11u = 33

Jill and Jerry have 33 plants altogether.

63

The ratio of Bill's money to Bunny's money was 2 : 3. After Bunny spent $\frac{1}{2}$ of her money, Bill had $43 more than Bunny. How much money did Bunny have in the end?

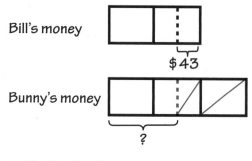

a. 2 X $43 = $86

b. $86 + $43 = $129

In the end, Bunny had $129.

64

The ratio of Toni's money to Rebecca's money was 5 : 8. Rebecca had $51.30 more than Toni. When Rebecca spent some of her money on a new outfit, she reduced her funds by $\frac{3}{4}$. Does Rebecca have enough money left to buy a white beret that costs $29.95?

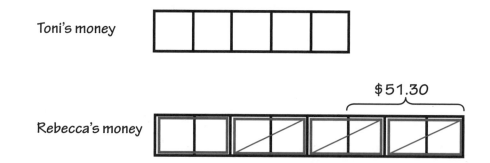

? = Does Rebecca have enough money left to buy a beret for $29.95?

3u = $51.30
1u = $17.10
2u = $34.20

Rebecca has enough money left to buy the beret.

65

Mike had $80 and Dolly had $65. Then they went out to lunch, and each paid $\frac{1}{2}$ of the bill. After they paid for lunch, the ratio of Mike's money to Dolly's money was 7 : 4. How much was their lunch bill?

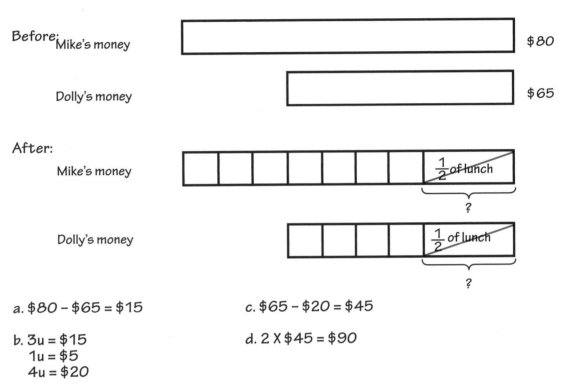

a. $80 − $65 = $15

b. 3u = $15
   1u = $5
   4u = $20

c. $65 − $20 = $45

d. 2 X $45 = $90

Their lunch bill was $90. (Wow! I hope it was good!)

66

Althea's and Bing's money totaled $23.76; the ratio of Althea's money to Bing's was 3 to 8. The ratio of Chanise's money to Bing's was 5 to 6. How much more money did Bing have than Chanise?

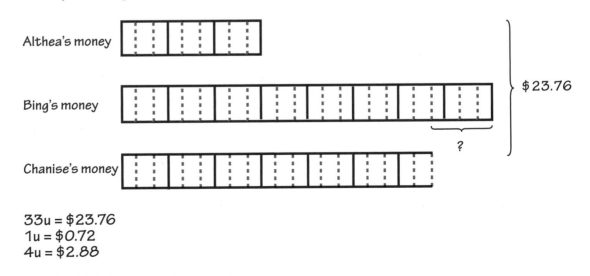

33u = $23.76
1u = $0.72
4u = $2.88

Bing had $2.88 more than Chanise.

74

Initially, of all the members of the school band, 30% were boys. After some of the boys dropped out, only 20% of the remaining band members were boys. If the band had 80 members in the beginning, how many boys left the band?

Before:

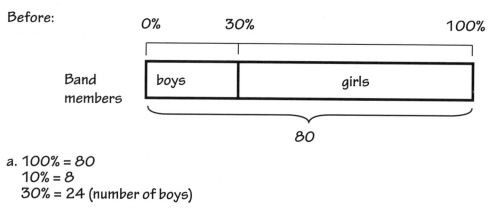

a. 100% = 80
   10% = 8
   30% = 24 (number of boys)

b. 80 – 24 = 56 (number of girls)

After:

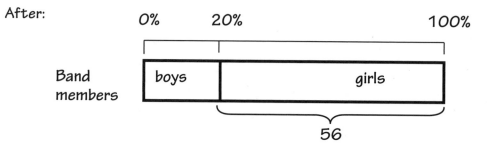

? = # of boys who left

c. 100% – 20% = 80%

d. 80% = 56
   10% = 7
   20% = 14

e. 24 – 14 = 10

Ten boys left the band.

75

Initially, there were 4,800 plants for sale at Walker Farm. Of those, 30% were annuals and the rest were perennials. By noon on Saturday, $\frac{2}{5}$ of the annuals had sold and 768 of the perennials had sold. What percent of the remaining plants were annuals?

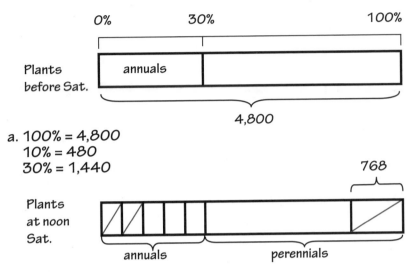

a. 100% = 4,800
   10% = 480
   30% = 1,440

? = % of remaining plants that were annuals

b. 5u = 1,440
   1u = 288
   3u = 864

c. 4,800 – 1,440 = 3,360

d. 3,360 – 768 = 2,592

e. 864 + 2,592 = 3,456

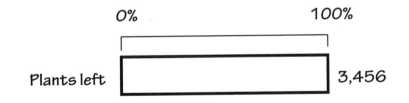

f. 100% = 3,456
   1% = 34.56

g. 864 ÷ 34.56 = 25

Of the remaining plants, 25% were annuals.

76

Carrie mailed 20% more holiday cards this year than she mailed last year. If she mailed 13 more cards this year than last year, how many did she mail last year?

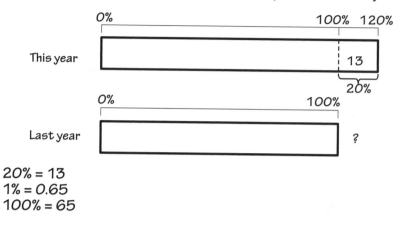

20% = 13
1% = 0.65
100% = 65

Carrie mailed 65 holiday cards last year.

77

At first Priscilla had 5 times as many jellybeans as Camilla. Then the girls decided to share some with their friend Scarlett. After Priscilla gave Scarlett 12% of her jellybeans and Camilla gave Scarlett 25% of hers, Scarlett had a total of 102 jellybeans. That was 50% more than what she started with. How many jellybeans did Camilla give Scarlett?

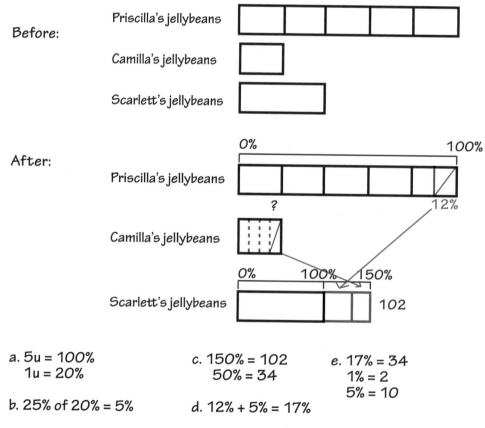

a. 5u = 100%
   1u = 20%

b. 25% of 20% = 5%

c. 150% = 102
   50% = 34

d. 12% + 5% = 17%

e. 17% = 34
   1% = 2
   5% = 10

Camilla gave Scarlett 10 jellybeans.

83

At the Corner Market, 3 oranges and 1 apple cost $1.86, and 2 oranges and 3 apples cost $2.15. Find the cost of 1 apple.

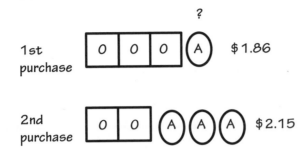

a. Double the first purchase and triple the second purchase.

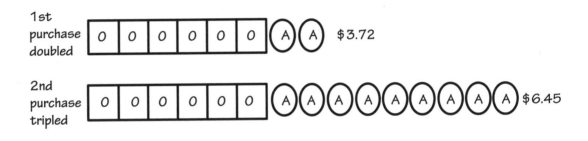

b. Subtract the first model from the second.
$6.45 – $3.72 = $2.73

7A = $2.73
1A = $0.39

One apple costs $0.39.

Model Drawing for Challenging Word Problems

84

The sum of 2 whole numbers is 28. When one of the numbers is tripled and added to the other number, the sum is then 50. What are the 2 numbers?

Step 1:

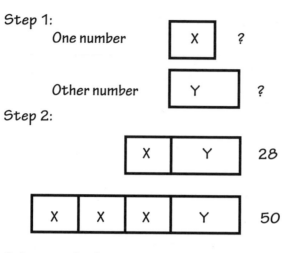

One number   [X]   ?

Other number   [Y]   ?

Step 2:

| X | Y | 28

| X | X | X | Y | 50

Subtract the first model from the second.
50 – 28 = 22

2X = 22
1X = 11
28 – 11 = 17

The 2 numbers are 11 and 17.

85

Soren and Cassie each donated the same amount of money to NPR. Before they made their donations, Soren had $178 and Cassie had $670. After donating, Cassie had 5 times as much money as Soren. How much money did they each donate?

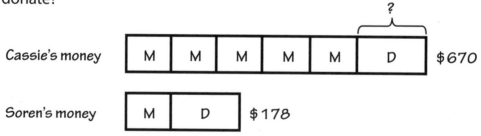

Cassie's money | M | M | M | M | M | D | $670

Soren's money | M | D | $178

a. Subtract the second model from the first.
   $670 – $178 = $492
   4M = $492
   1M = $123

b. $178 – $123 = $55

Cassie and Soren each donated $55.

86

Kate and Melissa both went to the same store to buy eggs and bread for their families. Kate bought 3 dozen eggs and 5 loaves of bread; she spent $30.07. Melissa purchased 2 dozen eggs and 2 loaves of bread; she spent $14.74. What is the store charging for a dozen eggs?

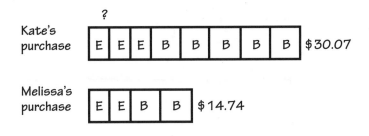

a. Double Kate's purchase and triple Melissa's purchase.

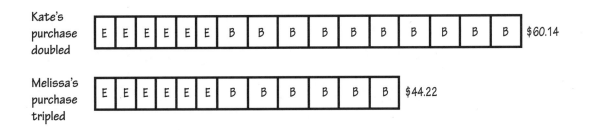

b. Subtract the second model from the first.
   $60.14 – $44.22 = $15.92

   4B = $15.92
   1B = $3.98

c. 2B = $7.96

d. $14.74 – $7.96 = $6.78

e. 2E = $6.78
   1E = $3.39

The store is charging $3.39 for a dozen eggs.

Model Drawing for Challenging Word Problems

89

Inese had collected 120 recipes. Once she got *r* more from a friend, she then had twice as many as Sharon. How many recipes does Sharon have? Express your answer in terms of *r*.

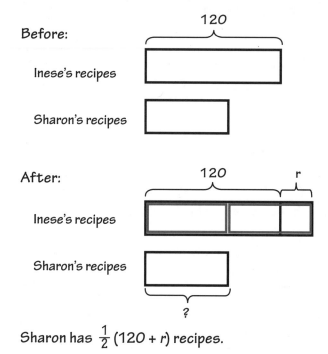

Before:

Inese's recipes

Sharon's recipes

After:

Inese's recipes

Sharon's recipes

?

Sharon has $\frac{1}{2}(120 + r)$ recipes.

90

Gerry divided his Porsche model cars equally into 4 sets. If each set ended up with *k* cars, how many cars did he have? Express your answer in terms of *k*.

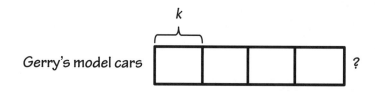

k

Gerry's model cars

?

Gerry had 4*k* cars.

91

If $\frac{2}{3}$ of a number is *m*, what is the number? Express your answer in terms of *m*.

m

The number

?

The number is $1\frac{1}{2}$ *m*.

92

Char took her friends out for ice cream. Her friends ordered 5 cones for $3.25 each and one sundae for $y. If Char gave the waitress $40, how much change did she get back? Express your answer in terms of y.

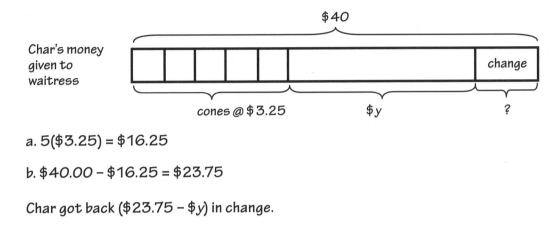

a. 5($3.25) = $16.25

b. $40.00 − $16.25 = $23.75

Char got back ($23.75 − $y) in change.

93

Terri won $250 playing bingo. She gave $b to each of her 3 friends. How much money did she have left? Express your answer in terms of b.

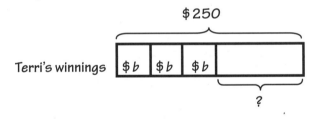

Terri had ($250 − $3b) left.

94

John had 28 books. His friend Kath had x times as many books as John. How many books did they have altogether? Express your answer in terms of x.

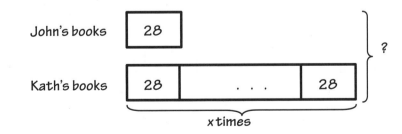

They had (28 + 28x) books altogether. This could also be written as 28(1 + x).

95

If Patt had *y* cookies and Flo had 2 cookies, Patt had how many times as many cookies as Flo? Express your answer in terms of *y*.

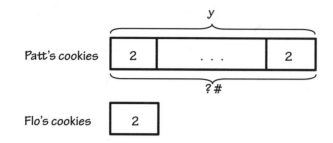

Patt had $\frac{y}{2}$ as many cookies as Flo.

96

Miguel bought 6 pounds of coffee. He gave the clerk $h and received $4.26 in change. How much per pound did the coffee cost? Express your answer in terms of *h*.

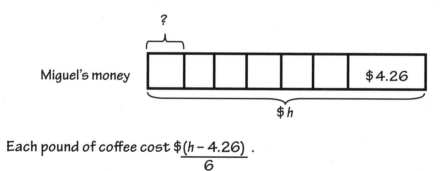

Each pound of coffee cost $\dfrac{(h - 4.26)}{6}$.

97

Betty has $5c. Jim has twice as much as Betty, and Laureen has $4 more than Jim. How much do they have altogether? Express your answer in terms of *c*.

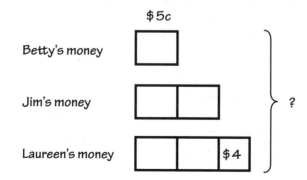

5($5c) = $25c

They have ($25c + $4) altogether.

Solutions for Final Exam Problems

1

The Majestic Theater has a seating capacity of 420. At a Saturday matinee $\frac{1}{4}$ of the seats were sold to adults, $\frac{2}{5}$ to senior citizens, and the rest to children. If the management sold all the seats that day, how many children's tickets did they sell?

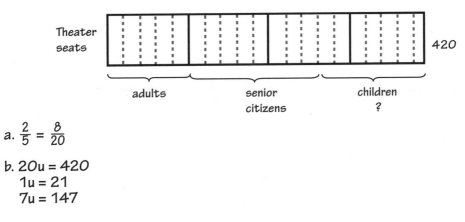

a. $\frac{2}{5} = \frac{8}{20}$

b. 20u = 420
   1u = 21
   7u = 147

They sold 147 children's tickets.

2

Find 3 consecutive odd integers such that twice the first number is equal to 17 more than the third number.

Step 1:

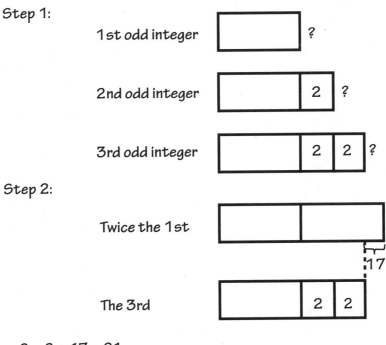

Step 2:

a. 2 + 2 + 17 = 21
   1u = 21

b. 21 + 2 = 23
   21 + 4 = 25

The numbers are 21, 23, and 25.

Model Drawing for Challenging Word Problems

3

The sum of Cathy's and Tony's ages is 65. Eight years ago Cathy's age was $\frac{2}{5}$ of Tony's age. How old are they now?

Ages now:

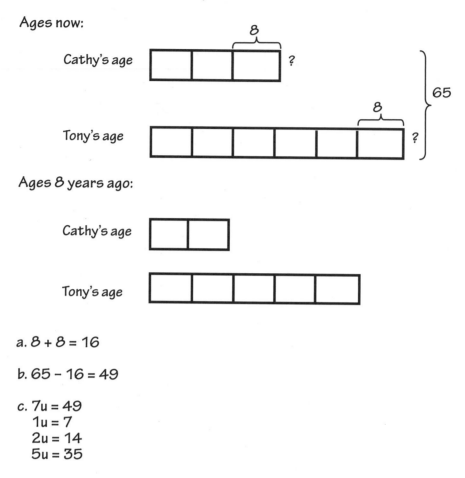

Ages 8 years ago:

a. 8 + 8 = 16

b. 65 – 16 = 49

c. 7u = 49
   1u = 7
   2u = 14
   5u = 35

d. 14 + 8 = 22
   35 + 8 = 43

Cathy is 22 years old and Tony is 43.

4

Tim loved hot dogs and bought 5 of them at the hot dog stand. If he gave the owner $h and got $12.05 in change, what was the cost of a single hot dog? Express your answer in terms of h.

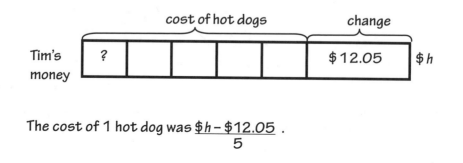

The cost of 1 hot dog was $\underline{\dfrac{\$h - \$12.05}{5}}$.

5 Travis has $\frac{1}{5}$ as many books as Manda and $\frac{2}{3}$ as many books as Dan. If Dan has 7 more books than Travis, how many books does Manda have?

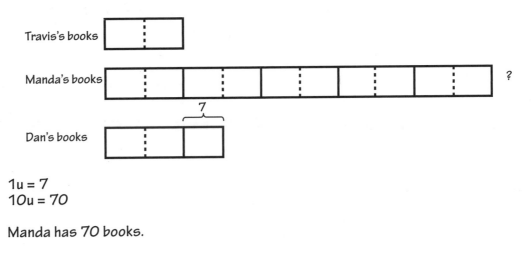

1u = 7
10u = 70

Manda has 70 books.

6 Beck had $5 less than Delmar. After Beck went shopping for new clothes and spent $\frac{2}{3}$ of her money, she then had $35 less than Delmar. How much money did Beck have left?

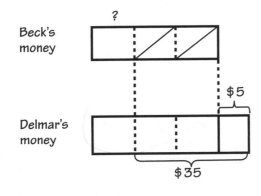

a. $35 – $5 = $30

b. 2u = $30
   1u = $15

Beck had $15 left.

7

Originally, Barbie and Maggie had the same number of plants in their homes. After Barbie gave away 17 plants and 5 of Maggie's died, the ratio of Barbie's plants to Maggie's plants was 4 : 7. How many plants did they each start with?

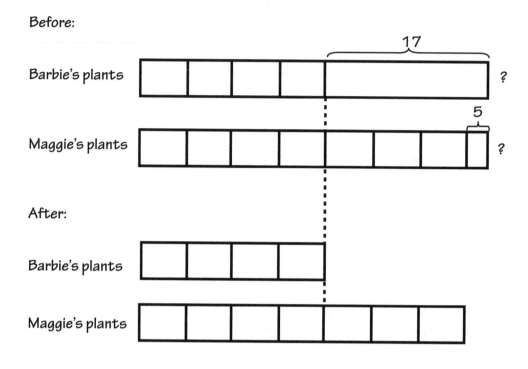

Before:

Barbie's plants

Maggie's plants

After:

Barbie's plants

Maggie's plants

a. 17 – 5 = 12

b. 3u = 12
   1u = 4
   4u = 16

c. 16 + 17 = 33

Barbie and Maggie each started with 33 plants.

8

The sales team at Latti Motors sold 2 used cars on Monday. One car sold for $3,800, which resulted in a profit of 25% over the buying price. The other car sold for $2,480, which represented a 20% loss. Find the total loss or profit from these 2 sales.

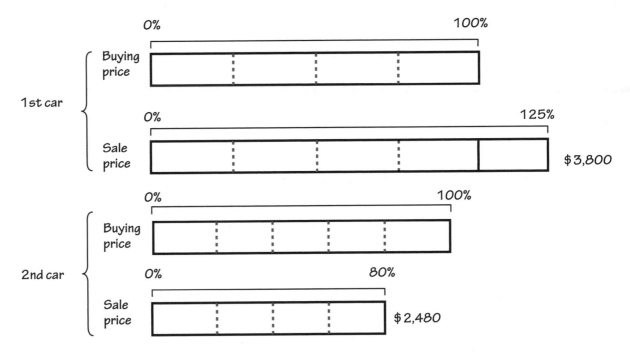

? = Profit – loss

a. Profit:
   5u = $3,800
   1u = $760

b. Loss:
   4u = $2,480
   1u = $620

c. $760 – $620 = $140

The 2 sales resulted in a profit of $140.

9

Meg, Zach, and Josh all had summer jobs. During the first week of the summer, the ratio of Meg's earnings to Zach's earnings was 5 : 12. The comparison of Zach's and Josh's earnings was 3 : 2. If Meg ended up with $21 less than Zach that week, how much did Josh earn during the same week?

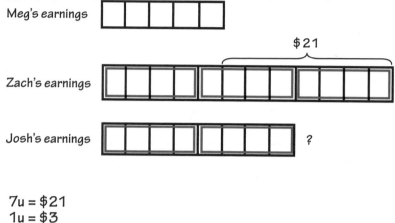

$7u = \$21$
$1u = \$3$
$8u = \$24$

Josh earned $24 during the first week of the summer.

During the Pie Challenge at the County Fair, a total of 50 apple and blueberry pies were entered into the contest. Initially the ratio of apple pies to blueberry pies was 4 : 1. Later the judges disqualified some of the blueberry pies, leaving 5 times as many apple pies as blueberry pies to be judged. How many blueberry pies were disqualified?

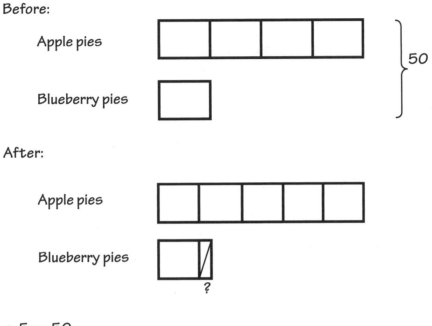

Before:

Apple pies

Blueberry pies

} 50

After:

Apple pies

Blueberry pies

?

a. 5u = 50
   1u = 10
   4u = 40

b. 5a = 40
   1a = 8

c. 10 − 8 = 2

Two blueberry pies were disqualified.

Print Resources

Forsten, Char. 2009. *Step-by-step model drawing*. Peterborough, NH: Crystal Springs Books.

Lee, Peng Yee, ed. 2009. *Teaching primary school mathematics*. Singapore: McGraw-Hill.

Ministry of Education, Singapore. 2009. *The Singapore model method for learning mathematics*. Singapore: Panpac Education.

Polya, G. 2004. *How to solve it*. Princeton, NJ: Princeton University Press.

Yoong, Wong Khoon, et. al, eds. 2009. *Mathematics education*. Singapore: World Scientific Publishing Co. Pte. Ltd.

Helpful Websites

Crystal Springs Books: www.SDE.com/crystalsprings
Model-drawing workbooks, professional books, and manipulatives

National Council of Teachers of Mathematics: www.nctm.org
Lists of curriculum standards and focal points

The Singapore Maths Teacher: www.thesingaporemaths.com
Help for teachers learning model drawing

Staff Development for Educators: www.SDE.com
Singapore Math information, resources, links, placement tests; conferences, seminars, and online courses for professional development

Thinking Blocks: www.thinkingblocks.com
Free, interactive website for learning and practicing model drawing

Index

Note: Page numbers in *italics* refer to reproducibles.